Guarding Your Family's Health

ⅅ The Danbury Press

WOMAN ALIVE

Guarding Your Family's Health

by Mary Senechal

Inter
i
bérica, S.A. de Ediciones

Series Coordinator: John Mason
Design Director: Guenther Radtke
Picture Editor: Peter Cook
Copy Editor: Damian Grint
Research: Ann Fisher
        Marian Pullen
Consultants: Beppie Harrison
        Jo Sandilands

Contents

Few things are more important to a mother than knowing how to keep her family—and herself—in the very best of health. That doesn't just mean protecting the family from illness and coping if they do get sick, but achieving the positive health of mind and body that is the key to a family's well-being. This book is designed to help you care for all these aspects of your family's health. Here is practical advice on watching out for your husband's health—when he won't; on tackling stress; handling teenage troubles; nursing a sick child; caring for an elderly relative; when to call the doctor—and what to do until he arrives; family emergencies—and how to cope; the drugs that should be in your medicine chest—and the ones that shouldn't. Here, above all, is a guide to healthier, happier living for your family—and yourself.

What is a Family?

Throughout the ages, in every society, the family has been a major factor, not only in ensuring human survival, but in shaping the personal happiness of each one of its members.

Below: even among early peoples, like these primitive Indians of Brazil, the family has always been a central part of community life.

Right: in the 1500's, religious beliefs and codes of inheritance reinforced the natural ties of love and kinship that bound a family together.

Below: to the Victorians, the moral values of family life were paramount, and family loyalties for them extended to the most distant relatives.

Above right: close ties with the wider family are still important in Spain, where a family gathering is always good cause for celebration.

Above: the smaller modern family continues to be an important source of emotional support.

The Family Doctor

Every culture has had its healers, men who sought to cure by magic or by medicine, but whose greatest skill often lay in giving a sick person the longed-for reassurance that his pain could be allayed and his health restored again.

Below: a medicine man of the Blackfoot tribe. Ritual dress and ceremony were an important aspect of his art, but he could set broken bones, and knew the value of herbal remedies.

Right: patients of the late 1500's line up for treatment. Blood is taken from the first man's arm, in the belief that this would draw the disease out of his body and so effect a cure.

Below: the witch-doctor relies on incantations, magic potions, and elaborate ritual to drive out the evil spirits thought to have caused an illness.

Right: doctors are sometimes made fun of, too. Here is a satirical look at a doctor of the 1600's, complete with giant-sized syringe.

Above right: Australia's flying doctor service brings emergency medical assistance to sick people in the remotest corners of the country.

Below: thanks to advances in medical knowledge and training, the patient of today's doctor can be sure of being in good hands.

Folk Remedies

Age-old beliefs in the healing properties of herbs, charms, and other traditional folk remedies include a fascinating mixture of myth, superstition, and, in some cases, scientific fact.

Right: nearly 2,000 years ago, the Roman naturalist Pliny noted the medicinal value of pastes and potions made from the willow tree. Today, we know he was right. Willow bark is the basic ingredient of our widely-used aspirin.

Above: many curious remedies have been proposed for warts. The application of frogs, fresh rainwater, copper coins, or a live snail—as shown here—have all been tried as cures.

Right: a 12th-century herbal shows foxglove, which we continue to use in treating heart disease, and camomile, still brewed into a tea to soothe the nerves and ease digestion pains.

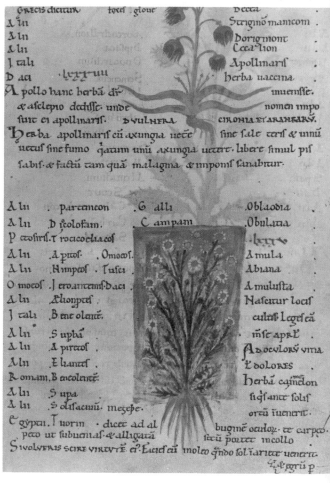

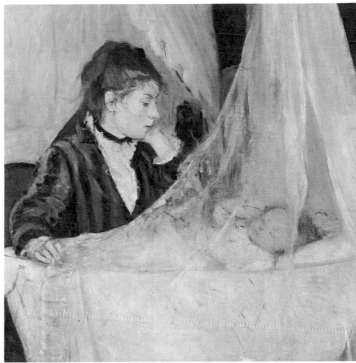

Below: the Amish, a group of Pennsylvania Dutch who cling to their traditional belief in folk medicine. Amish remedies include cow dung for inflammations, and the wearing of a pig's eye-tooth to keep rheumatism at bay.

Above: mother's lullaby has its origin in the ancient legend of Lilith, the demon of illness-inducing draughts, who was thought to enter a baby's stomach and cause colic. The lullaby was sung to make the fiendish Lilith stay away.

Progress to Health

The dramatic medical advances of recent times can promise us longer and healthier lives than were ever dreamed of as possible in the past.

Below left: with no knowledge to guide them, doctors of plague victims in 1665 tried to avoid infection by wearing a spice-filled mask and using a stick instead of hands to touch patients.

Below right: early hospitals, like this one in Renaissance Italy, made a start toward providing more organized treatment of the sick.

Right: the discovery, in 1796, that a virus from cows could prevent smallpox was at first greeted with ridicule. A cartoon pictures the vaccine turning people who took it into cows.

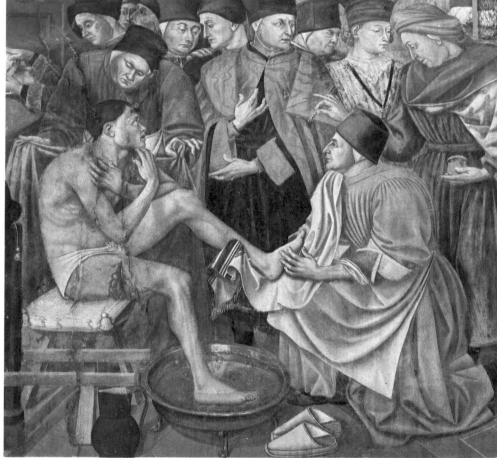

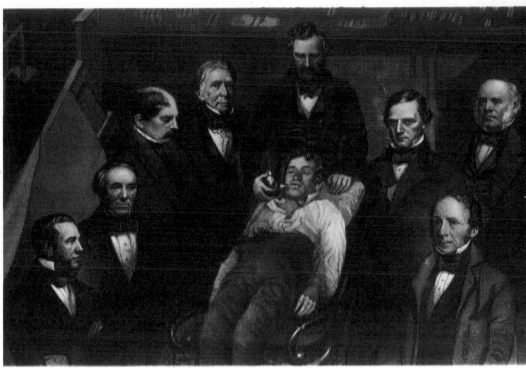

Below left: following in the footsteps of Florence Nightingale, who set up a school for them in 1860, came women nurses like this one of 1911—well-trained, efficient, and neat.

Above: the development of anesthetics paved the way for the pain-free surgery of today. **Below:** doctor and nurses care for a young patient in a well-equipped modern hospital.

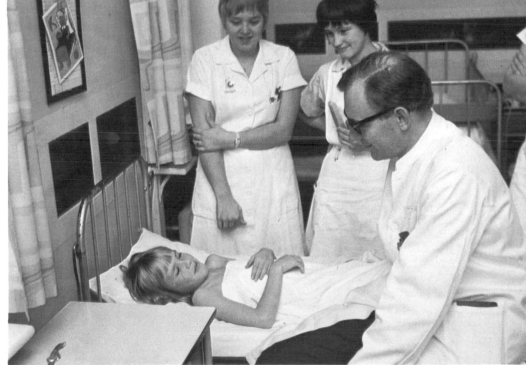

Their Need for You

Gone are the days of the Victorian Mama who was often a remote figure in her children's lives. Mama has become Mommy, personally concerned with every aspect of her children's upbringing, and aware of their need for her love and acceptance to help them grow into physically and emotionally healthy adults.

Above: a Victorian print shows nanny presenting her small charges to their parents before dinner, often the only time in the day that the children would get a chance to see mother.

Above: a moment of quiet intimacy between mother and daughter, captured on canvas.

Right: the anxious concern of a mother as she watches by her sick child's bed, depicted by a woman artist in this painting done in 1865.

Above right: grandmother finds comfort in knowing that she is still needed and loved.
Below right: a young mother today aims to understand, respect, and enjoy her children.

Your Family's Health

1

When a family is healthy, it shows. And that good-health glow comes from a sense of emotional well-being as well as physical health. The family has a vital role to play in ensuring the emotional health of all its members, parents and children alike.

Your fretful baby has kept you awake all night long. Your three-year-old has just thumped neighbor Johnny on the head with a toy train. Your teenage daughter is threatening to leave home. Your husband is slumped gloomily over his bank statement. No one needs to tell you that life in a family taxes every ounce of energy and skill you've got.

Family life is like national life in miniature. Families are made up of individuals, each with his own personality, rights, and requirements. What's more, no family is ever the same from one year to the next. Patterns within the family are constantly changing as each child grows, or new babies are born, and as parents mature and change, too. Each family member is different. Each has his own special needs. And no matter how much aid the modern family may get from outside, most of the responsibility for running this mini-state falls on you. As the mother of a family, you have to bear in mind the needs of your husband, your children, your relatives—and yourself—not to mention dealing with the budget, the cooking, the shopping, and the housework, all at once. So, where are the rewards in this amazing job? Just where you might least expect to find them. For the more complex the daily interaction of family life becomes, the more it can enrich the individual life of each one of its members—including you.

Belonging to a family gives parents and children alike a unique sense of their own individual worth. No matter what happens to us in the world outside we know that there is one place where we can relax and be our true selves. We know that there is one group in which we are loved and accepted. And that knowledge is a source of inner strength against all the challenges and disappointments that life may cast our way. If we are sure of our family's love, we will have the confidence we need to take on our responsibilities, to form new relationships, and to lead fuller lives.

All these good things don't just happen in families. They need care and thought. Guiding your family toward a healthy, satisfying life goes beyond providing the care and protection that your husband and children need for good physical health. It means providing for their emotional well-being, too.

For a family to have emotional health, each of its members must feel loved and cherished for himself. Happy family life is founded on the kind of love that accepts and values each member, not for doing, but simply for being. It is this unquestioning love that makes a home into a haven for parents, and contributes in large measures to the healthy development of their children. "The failure to convince the growing child that this is the feeling his parents have for him," says New York pediatrician Dr. William Homan, "is probably the single most important cause of future personality deviations in later childhood, in adolescence, and in adulthood."

Telling parents to love their children may seem ridiculous. Most parents do love their children, and love them in the very non-critical way Dr. Homan is talking about. But they may, quite unwittingly, fail to let their children know the way they feel. Some parents may be afraid of spoiling their children. Others may be so anxious to help their youngsters "stand up for themselves" in a competitive world that they push them too hard, and appear to value a child's achievements more than the child himself.

Uncritical love doesn't mean letting discipline go by the board. But it does mean drawing a clear distinction between disapproval of a child's misbehavior and disapproval of the child himself. Surprising though it may seem, this distinction can be the key to growing self-discipline. For the more a child is convinced of his parents' love and acceptance of him, the more important their occasional disapproval of his actions will be.

Each child is a unique individual with his own special needs and reactions. By trying to better understand what makes your child tick, and by recognizing his natural strengths and limitations, you can help him to develop the inner resources that he needs to realize his potential.

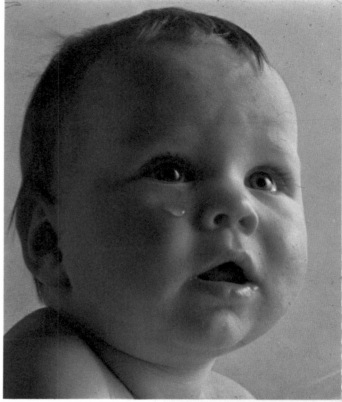

18

Love won't make your child soft. On the contrary, it will give him the strength he needs to become independent. His ability to move into new groups, take on new responsibilities, and face the challenges of adult life is rooted in the confidence that comes from being accepted and loved by his family.

Loving your children doesn't mean treating them all equally. Each child's personality is unique—different from you, different from your husband, and different from his brothers and sisters. And each child's place within the family will only be secure if his individual rights and requirements are recognized. Sensitive Ellen, for example, may want lots of gentle encouragement, while her brother Henry needs a firm hand. As child expert Dr. Simon Yudkin puts it, "Each child needs, not equal treatment, but equal opportunity for his full development."

Your children aren't the only ones who need that opportunity, You need it, too. Remember, you're a person in your own right as well as a mother, and you can't help your children develop as individuals if you sacrifice your own individuality along the way. No matter how great the demands of family life, it's important to find time to keep up with your friends, to follow your own interests, and to share moments alone with your husband. This will mean enlisting your family's cooperation but it's well worth the effort. A mother who feels fulfilled herself will do a lot to promote the well-being of those closest to her.

For some women, this will mean taking a job outside the home. For others, it will mean building a personal life within the framework of the family. To work or not to work is a decision that each woman must make for herself—unless, of course, the state of the

household budget makes it for her. You are not selfish to want to protect your own individuality. Nor are you less of a person if you prefer the role of full-time housewife and mother. Only you can judge what is best for your health and happiness, and so for the health and happiness of your family.

Whether or not a woman goes out to work, she and her husband must share as equal partners in the task of family leadership. Of course, they won't always see eye-to-eye about each other's parenting. After all, husband and wife are two separate individuals, who have been brought up differently themselves, and who have already lived a good part of their lives in different environments. But so long as they can agree on their basic approach to raising their children, these very differences can

make them a well-balanced team, with each parent bringing his own unique contribution to the lives of their children.

No matter how well parents may agree, the family circle will not always roll along at a cheerful, even pace. Among those who are close, quarrels are bound to arise, and feelings can be deeply hurt. There are bound to be times when you lose your temper, when you feel tired or irritable and find your children a trial. But a united family can take such moments in its stride. As the children grow older, they will come to understand some of the pressures you face. They will begin to consider your feelings as well as their own, and you may sometimes find their thoughtfulness coming to your rescue on just those days when you need it most.

This kind of support is one of the chief assets of family life. In his family, each member has a vital outlet for his feelings – of joy as well as sorrow, of triumph as well as failure, of hostility as well as love. And the fact that he can "let off steam" at home, among those who love and believe in him, helps to protect him from the stresses of the outside world. "For emotional recharging," says Dr. Joan Gomez, author of *How Not to Die Young*, "every person needs a home: a place where he or she can find and cultivate strength for striving, courage for the acceptance of the inevitable, however unpleasant, and inner peace."

Today, more than ever, we need the qualities that family life can bring to all its members. Never has family life faced more pressures than it does today. Never has the task of parents seemed more challenging. But few parents would exchange that task for any other, because the rewards of success are measured in human happiness.

Guarding your family's health is a vital part of that task. It doesn't just mean coping when members of your family are sick, but helping them—and yourself—stay healthy and happy. It takes love, and it takes the knowledge to deal with the problems that are bound to arise at times in any family. You provide the love. This book will help to give you the kind of know-how you need to back it up.

Right: father's role in family life is just as important as mother's. Children need the love and guidance of both their parents, and each child should be able to spend some time alone with his mother and his father—a time when the two can share some special interest together, or simply get to know each other better.

Left: "Not in front of
the children" is the
wisest rule for parents
to follow when they
disagree on matters of
discipline. Differences of
opinion are best saved
for calm discussion later.
But if parents can agree
on their basic approach
to raising their children,
an occasional argument
need not mean disaster.

23

How to Have Healthy Children

2

Healthy children are a joy to behold. They are bright-eyed, energetic, and alert. They learn more easily, play more joyfully, meet challenges more readily, and enjoy life more. And they almost always grow into healthy adults.

Whatever their ages, children share the same basic health needs. Ensuring their good health means giving them a happy home, with the kind of food, exercise, rest, and protection that will help them grow well and stay well.

Every child charts his own unique course on the road to growth. And rarely will any two children reach the same milestones with equal speed. A perfectly healthy five-year-old may be 39 inches tall. Another may top the 46-inch mark. Weight at this age may range all the way from 31 to 51 pounds. No wonder it is so difficult to tell whether your child's size is "normal" for his age or not. The only really important thing is whether he seems active, fit, and happy. However, since children's growth does follow an overall pattern, standards for height and weight that allow for normal differences (see page 27), can give you a rough idea of how your particular child is likely to grow over the years.

Growth is not a steady process. Children grow rapidly at some times and slowly at others. During his first year, a baby grows sensationally fast, trebling his birth weight and adding about nine inches to his height. If he were to go on growing at this rate, he would end up being about half a mile tall. But after about one year, his growth slows down. Thus, a long baby will not necessarily grow into a tall adult. However, by the age of 18 months for girls and 2 years for boys, a child will already have reached about half his adult height. And a toddler who is heavier and taller than his companions will usually maintain his lead throughout childhood.

Generally speaking, ages 7 to 11 are the slowest growth period of all, but between 10 and 12, girls begin a growth spurt that puts them a couple of years ahead of boys. Boys have their growth spurt later, and although they may shoot up by as much as six inches in a single year, they generally go on growing for longer than girls, until they finally overtake their sisters once and for all.

A child's eventual size depends on many factors, including, of course, the body build he inherits from his parents. You want to know in advance how tall your child will grow? A simple piece of arithmetic will give you a clue. For a boy, add your height to your husband's, plus six inches, and divide by two. For a girl, subtract six inches from the combined heights before dividing.

Every mother knows that if a child is to grow strong and healthy, he needs the nourishment that comes from a well-balanced diet. This doesn't mean that you have to turn yourself into an expert nutritionist to figure out what your child should be eating. So long as you choose each day's meals from the seven food groups shown in the chart on page 28, you can be sure of giving your child all the nutrition he needs.

Getting your child to eat seven different types of food, two or three times a day, can seem like a monumental task. But it becomes a whole lot

Healthy children are happy children. Bright-eyed, shiny-haired, active, and alert, they make a picture of glowing good health that is one of the most rewarding tokens of a parent's love and care.

easier if you think of your child's diet on a weekly, rather than a daily basis. A child's diet doesn't have to be perfectly balanced *every* day. He might skip his vegetables one day and go overboard on meat and eggs instead. Next day he might drink quarts of milk and very little else. Another day, he may stick mainly to fruit and cereal. But, provided his overall diet from week to week contains some food from each of the various groups, his nutritional requirements will be met. Bear in mind that all the foods within each food group are interchangeable, and that fruits can be safely substituted for vegetables. That way, you will see that even the most important foods can be replaced, and when a child refuses foods that are "good for him," you can come up with an equally nutritious substitute. If Susan dislikes eggs, she may eat cheese or meat instead. If she hates cooked vegetables, try offering her raw vegetable salad, or a glass of vegetable juice, or simply switch to fruit instead. If she won't drink milk, maybe she will take it in custard, puddings, or soup. And don't forget that there is the equivalent of one pint of milk in a couple of ounces of cheese.

Similarly, if your child will only eat one food from a particular group, there is no need to worry. The only meat Johnny wants is ground beef? Then there is no reason to insist he try something else. Lamb, or pork, or chicken, are not going to improve his diet just because they are different—especially if Johnny won't eat as much of them.

What about the foods that are not good for your child? These are easy to identify, too. Foods to keep to a minimum in your child's diet are those made with refined and bleached wheat flour, and refined rice, corn, and cereals or desserts made from these. Refined grains have lost most of their vitamins and protein, and even enriched white bread, with some vitamins restored to it, may fall short of wholewheat bread for food value. When you serve cereals and pasta, try to get the brands made from either whole grains or unbleached flour. Other foods to avoid are those containing large amounts of sugar (candies, chocolate, cakes, pastries, rich cookies, ice

Children can have a lot of fun measuring themselves—and who cares if the results aren't always too accurate? But if you do want to keep a record of your child's height, have him take off his shoes and stand with his back straight against the wall. Place a book flat on top of his head. Mark the place where the lower edge of the book is, and measure down from your mark to the floor. The child can then fill in his name and the date against the mark. Check the chart on the right for the average height and weight of boys and girls at different ages, along with the likely range listed as normal variation. But remember, this is only a rough guide. Each child grows at his own pace, and good health can't be measured in pounds and inches alone.

Height and Weight

BOYS

AGE	HEIGHT Average	Extremes	WEIGHT Average	Extremes
6 MONTHS	26 ins	24–28 ins	17 lbs	13– 22 lbs
1 YR	29 ins	27–31 ins	22 lbs	18– 28 lbs
18 MONTHS	32 ins	29–35 ins	26 lbs	21– 31 lbs
2 YRS	34 ins	31–37 ins	28 lbs	22– 34 lbs
3 YRS	37 ins	34–41 ins	32 lbs	25– 39 lbs
4 YRS	40 ins	36–43 ins	37 lbs	28– 45 lbs
5 YRS	42 ins	39–46 ins	41 lbs	31– 51 lbs
6 YRS	45 ins	41–49 ins	45 lbs	35– 56 lbs
7 YRS	47 ins	43–51 ins	49 lbs	38– 62 lbs
8 YRS	49 ins	45–54 ins	54 lbs	42– 68 lbs
9 YRS	51 ins	47–56 ins	59 lbs	46– 76 lbs
10 YRS	53 ins	49–58 ins	65 lbs	51– 85 lbs
11 YRS	55 ins	50–60 ins	71 lbs	56– 95 lbs
12 YRS	57 ins	52–63 ins	78 lbs	61–108 lbs
13 YRS	59 ins	53–65 ins	86 lbs	67–121 lbs
14 YRS	61 ins	56–68 ins	97 lbs	73–136 lbs
15 YRS	64 ins	58–70 ins	112 lbs	82–147 lbs
16 YRS	67 ins	61–72 ins	126 lbs	95–156 lbs

GIRLS

AGE	HEIGHT Average	Extremes	WEIGHT Average	Extremes
6 MONTHS	25 ins	24–27 ins	16 lbs	13– 20 lbs
1 YR	29 ins	27–31 ins	21 lbs	16– 26 lbs
18 MONTHS	31 ins	29–33 ins	24 lbs	19– 30 lbs
2 YRS	33 ins	31–36 ins	26 lbs	21– 33 lbs
3 YRS	37 ins	34–39 ins	31 lbs	24– 38 lbs
4 YRS	39 ins	36–42 ins	34 lbs	28– 46 lbs
5 YRS	42 ins	39–45 ins	39 lbs	32– 50 lbs
6 YRS	45 ins	41–48 ins	43 lbs	35– 55 lbs
7 YRS	47 ins	43–51 ins	47 lbs	38– 62 lbs
8 YRS	49 ins	45–53 ins	53 lbs	42– 70 lbs
9 YRS	51 ins	47–56 ins	58 lbs	46– 79 lbs
10 YRS	53 ins	48–58 ins	64 lbs	50– 90 lbs
11 YRS	55 ins	50–60 ins	72 lbs	56–102 lbs
12 YRS	58 ins	52–63 ins	81 lbs	61–103 lbs
13 YRS	60 ins	54–66 ins	91 lbs	69–125 lbs
14 YRS	62 ins	57–67 ins	102 lbs	78–136 lbs
15 YRS	63 ins	58–68 ins	111 lbs	87–146 lbs
16 YRS	64 ins	59–68 ins	117 lbs	94–155 lbs

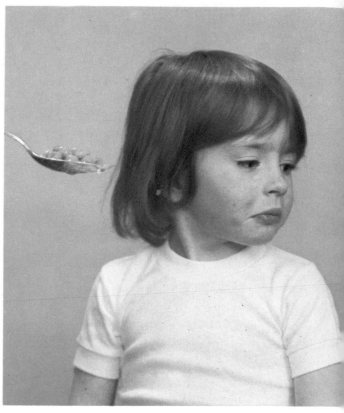

Above: the foods that children like most aren't always the ones that are best for their health. This little boy could happily eat his way through several ice creams but hates those nourishing peas. Below: a guide to healthy eating for all the family. Choose your week's meals from these groups, and be sure of giving them a well-balanced diet.

Weekly Food Guide

FOOD TYPE	SERVINGS REQUIRED PER WEEK			
	Child	Pre-teen and Teen	Adult	Aging Adult
*Milk or milk products (quarts)	5–7	7 or more	3–4 or more	3–4 or more
*Meat, fish, poultry, and eggs	10–12	20 or more	14 or more	14 or more
Green and yellow vegetables	10–12	14	14	at least 7
Citrus fruits and tomatoes	7	10–12	7	10–12
Potatoes, other fruits, and vegetables	7	7	7	3–4
Whole grain bread, flour, and cereal	24–25	25 or more	24–25	17–18
Butter or margarine (tablespoons)	14	21	17–18	10–12

*Cheese may be substituted for milk (1½ cups cottage cheese — 1 cup milk)
*Meat, fish, and poultry may be alternated with eggs or cheese, dried peas, beans, or lentils

cream, canned fruit, jellies, and jams), and all soft drinks or synthetic "fruit" juices.

Of course, an occasional cookie or ice cream is not going to bring about nutritional disaster. But a regular diet of sweetened or starchy foods can throw a child's natural instincts for choosing a healthy diet way off balance. He may go for such foods because they fill him up fast, but they will, in fact, give him practically no nourishment. And by spoiling his appetite for more valuable food-stuffs, they will deprive him of the proteins and vitamins he needs for health and growth.

Foods that are good for children are good for all the family, and the only adjustment you need to make for your children is in the amount you serve and the way you serve it. Even when children have a full set of first teeth, around the age of three, they cannot chew as well as adults, and will almost certainly prefer soft, moist meats to steaks or chops. Children do, however, like food that is varied in texture and color, so they often prefer their food in separate portions rather than as a casseroled mixture. Plan your desserts to be a nutritious part of the meal— fresh fruit, or a homemade custard, for example. Then, if your child spots his dessert and wants to eat it first, there will be no harm in letting him do just that. And when you are rushed for time, remember that cold meals are just as nutritious as hot ones.

What about eating between meals? Provided a child eats well at mealtimes, there is no reason to refuse him a snack in-between times. Some children do need food more often than three times a day. But snacks should be nutritious ones, like cheese, milk, raw vegetables, cold meat, or fruit. If your child is really hungry, he will enjoy these healthy extras. If he just wants to nibble cookies or candy for the sheer pleasure of it, he will turn down other foods, and you should be firm about refusing him a sweet snack.

Of course, you cannot stop your child from ever eating candies. But you can help prevent him from getting a "sweet tooth" if you give him candy only occasionally, particularly just after a meal when it will not spoil his appetite. If your child does not get into the habit of eating sweets when he is small, he probably won't be tempted by them later on. For extra insurance, however, you may like to keep your schoolchild's pocket money low enough to make him count what he spends on candy if he wants to buy other "treats" too.

How about the candies you can't control— the ones well-meaning relatives and friends offer him? This really depends on how often it happens. If Aunt Sarah brings over a big package of candies every Sunday afternoon, then it is wise to try and stop her. A once-monthly supply, kept in a special jar that the child knows is not going to be replenished for a while, could be a workable alternative. But if Grandma only visits you once or twice a year, you are sure to find it happier all around to let your child eat the candies she brings and to overlook his sugar intake for one day.

Remember, what your child eats is always more important than how much he eats. Food needs vary from child to child and from day to day, and the only certain guide to the amount a particular child needs at any given time is his own appetite.

Of course, you are bound to worry if your child does not seem to be eating well, and certainly you should report any prolonged loss of appetite to your doctor. You will probably find, however, that you just had not realized how much your child was actually eating or how much he really needs. This is especially likely during the second year of a child's life, when his appetite falls off considerably as his growth slows down. After all, as one pediatrician points out, if a child were to go on eating at the same rate as during his first year, he would weigh over 200 pounds by the time he was 10.

In his book *Child Sense,* Dr. William Homan suggests an excellent way of getting a toddler's food needs into perspective. First divide his weight into yours. Say you are about five times his size. So multiply what he eats by five. If he drinks ten ounces of milk a day, that is equivalent to three pints for you; if he eats one quarter of a sandwich, that equals one and a quarter sandwiches for you. And so on.

In spite of all this, you may still feel that your

The seemingly boundless energy and vigor of a healthy child leave the average adult way behind. Through sports and active play, children get the exercise they need for growth as well as general good health.

child is a poor eater. It is very hard to keep an open mind about what our loved ones eat, because children tend to equate food with love —and so do their mothers. When a child refuses the food his mother has prepared, she may unconsciously feel that he is rejecting her love, too, and react by trying to force him to eat. This can result in a daily round of food battles, with the child eating less and less, as his mother grows more and more anxious. So try to resist the temptation to coax or bribe your child to eat. Simply give him his food, and leave him to eat it while you get busy with something else. And eat it he will, just as soon as he realizes that no one is going to make a fuss over his appetite.

A much more serious problem is the child who eats too much. He, too, may be using food as a substitute for love, because he feels lonely or neglected. It is therefore wise to make sure that such a child gets lots of attention throughout the day and has plenty of happy occupations apart from eating, to keep him busy.

There are, of course, other reasons why a child may overeat. Maybe he has been encouraged to eat more than he needs, or possibly he has a taste for eating too many of the wrong kinds of food. Whatever the reason, overeating is bound to upset his natural weight controlling mechanism and make him overweight. And this is a serious hazard to his health and happiness.

Life can be sheer misery for a fat child. He may be teased unmercifully by his 'friends', left out of games at school, and become painfully self-conscious. The fat child is in physical danger, too. Eighty per cent of fat children grow into fat adults—the most likely victims of heart disease, respiratory infections,

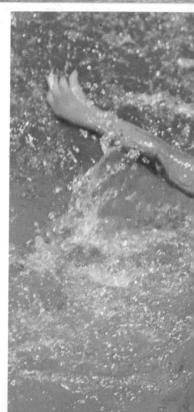

30

Above: some TV programs make frightening viewing, and exciting programs just before bed can make it harder for a child to sleep. Wise parents will share their children's viewing sometimes, keeping track of what they watch, and making a pact about the time to turn off the TV and get ready for bed.

Right: regular bedtimes are best, so that children—and parents—get sufficient rest, but sleep needs may vary widely from one child to another. Below: these 24-hour clocks will give you some idea of the *average* hours slept by children of different ages, including daytime naps for tots.

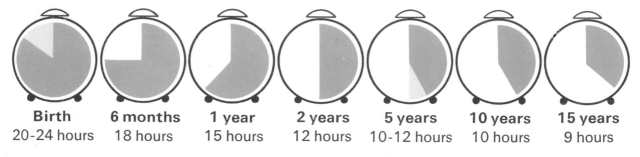

Birth	**6 months**	**1 year**	**2 years**	**5 years**	**10 years**	**15 years**
20-24 hours	18 hours	15 hours	12 hours	10-12 hours	10 hours	9 hours

diabetes, and arthritis. So, if your child appears too plump, do not be tempted to think that he will "grow out of it." Maybe he will—but there is no harm in making sure that he does.

Your attitude is the key to helping your plump child lose weight. It is vital to show him that you love him, and that you want to help him diet for his own good. Unless he is convinced of your love and support, all your attempts to help him lose weight will fail.

The next step is to take a careful look at what your child is eating, and gradually cut out all snacks, fried foods, sweets, and starches. At mealtimes, give him plenty of protein, fruit (except bananas), and vegetables (except potatoes, peas, and baked or lima beans). Allow him no more than one quart of milk a

day, and limit bread to three slices or less. Try to arrange for everyone in the family to have the same menu at mealtimes, so that he won't see others having foods that he can't share.

For the sake of his health, the child should not lose more than one pound a week, but since he is growing, he should gradually become slimmer and taller. And you will probably find that, by the end of two or three months, his weight will have dropped to near normal for his age and height. Above all, support the child's efforts to diet with lots of praise and encouragement—and by the example of your own eating habits. And continue to keep him on a healthy diet even when he has lost a satisfactory amount of weight. If, in spite of all your efforts, the child continues to

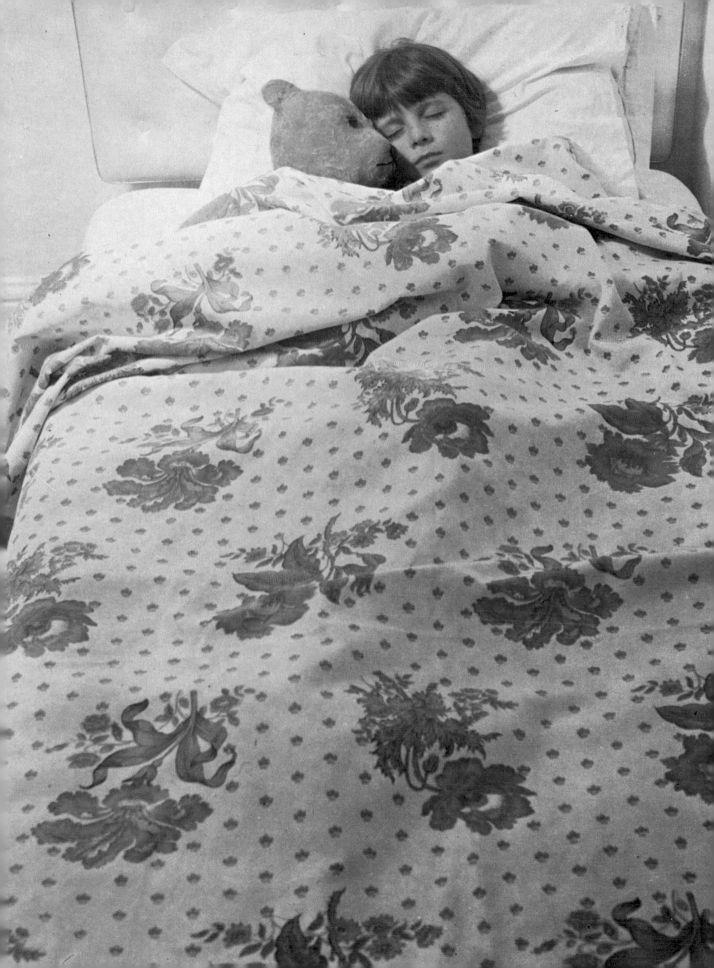

Below: one of a child's first visits to the doctor will probably be for a routine immunization, a vital step in protecting him from potential illness. Here is a typical immunization schedule, including injections, and booster shots where necessary, plus regular tests for tuberculosis. Immunization against diphtheria, tetanus, and pertussis (whooping cough) is given in a combined injection known as DTP. Material to combat polio may be added to this, or given separately by Sabin or Trivalent vaccine. TD is a tetanus-diphtheria recall injection

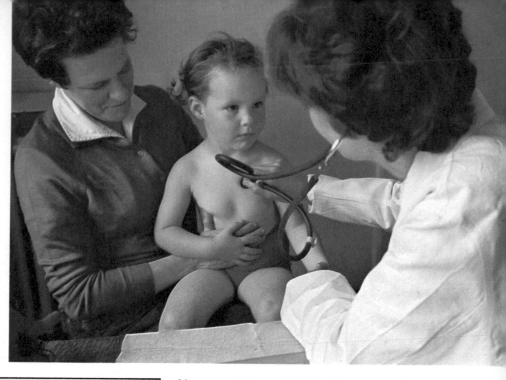

Immunization

2–3 months	DTP, Sabin Type 1 or Trivalent
3–4 months	DTP, Sabin Type 3 or Trivalent
4–5 months	DTP, Sabin Type 2 or Trivalent
9–11 months	Tuberculin Test
12 months	Measles Vaccine
12–24 months	Smallpox Vaccination, Mumps Vaccine, German Measles Vaccine
15–18 months	DTP, Trivalent Sabin
2 years	Tuberculin Test
3 years	DTP, Tuberculin Test
4 years	Tuberculin Test
6 years	TD, Smallpox Vaccination, Tuberculin Test, Trivalent Sabin
8 years	Tuberculin Test, Mumps Vaccine (if not given earlier or if child did not have mumps)
12 years	TD, Smallpox Vaccine, Tuberculin Test
14 years	Tuberculin Test
16 years	Tuberculin Test

Above: regular medical checkups are an important part of good health care throughout childhood. A toddler may find them a bit frightening at first, so it is comforting to have mother close at hand. Right: learning what the doctor does and the kind of instruments he uses can help children conquer their fears when it is their turn to be examined.

gain excessively, you should, of course, seek the advice of your doctor.

Good eating habits and a well-balanced diet will help your child build a strong and healthy body. But muscles, and the bones they affect, also grow by moving, and they can only develop properly if a child gets sufficient exercise. This doesn't mean spending a fortune on sports supplies. More important is having a place to play safely out of doors. If you do not have a yard, maybe there is a community playground your child could use, or perhaps you could get together with other parents to find a suitable play area, at a local school, for example.

Encourage your child to be interested in sports, and play with him if you can—it will do you both good. By the age of 9 or 10, however, a youngster will probably prefer team games with his own pals, and Dad should not feel too hurt if Johnny no longer admires his batting style. Remember, the more a child enjoys taking part in sports, the less likely he is to opt for spending most of his free time lounging

around indoors in front of the television set.

Running, walking, playing, and learning are pretty strenuous work for a child, and after a busy day, he needs plenty of sleep to restore his energies. Just how many hours of sleep he needs, no one can say for sure. Sleeping patterns, like eating patterns, vary from child to child, and are established even before a baby is born. Scientists in Rochester, Minn., who studied the sleep habits of two and three-year-olds, discovered that some children slept for as many as 17 hours a day, while others managed quite happily on 8. In general, lively children seem to need less sleep than placid types.

No matter what their individual sleep needs, however, all children should have plenty of rest, and it is wise to put them to bed at a reasonable hour even if they do not · fall asleep for a while. Toys will keep young children amused, and from about the age of 7, a child will probably enjoy reading in bed until he feels sleepy. That way, he will be getting valuable physical rest, and you and your

husband will also have a chance to relax by yourselves.

No healthy, happy child enjoys going to bed. But you can avoid too many bedtime battles by a little advance strategy. Right from babyhood, you should make it a rule not to bring the child out of his bedroom after bedtime, but give him any attention he needs in his own room. Once he is over six months old, be firm about resisting any calls for attention—one brief check to see that nothing is wrong should be your limit. In the case of an older child, try not to fall for those endless requests for a glass of water, or any other ingenious excuses to get you into the bedroom. And if Jimmy gets out of bed, march him firmly back again—no matter how cute he looks standing at the door clutching his teddy bear. Of course, all this applies when your child is perfectly well and healthy. If your child is awake and crying with earache, or is in the midst of a bout of measles, for example, then he obviously needs you there to help and comfort him, and an occasional night of cuddling while he is ill is certainly not going to spoil his normal sleeping habits.

Your child will fall asleep more easily if he does not play boisterous games or watch exciting TV programs just before bed. Make sure, too, that his bedroom is quiet and well-ventilated, and has a light he can turn on easily if he gets frightened during the night. If your child is an early waker, you will find it helps to leave toys and books beside his bed to keep him busy first thing in the morning.

What about the child who has nightmares? These are commonest in the 4 to 10 age group, and they, too, definitely warrant an exception to the "no visits after bedtime" rule. If a child wakes screaming from a frightening dream, cuddle and comfort him until he seems reassured, but don't take him into your own bed. He will quickly get a taste for that treat, and bed is one place where you and your husband have a right to privacy.

Frequent nightmares are a sign of physical or emotional distress. Perhaps your child is ill or starting an infection. Maybe he is having too much excitement during the day. Are frightening TV programs or bedtime stories disturbing his sleep? Is he anxious about school? Whatever the cause, you must try to track it down, with your doctor's help if necessary.

Sleepwalking, too, may be a sign of illness or anxiety, but occasional sleepwalking is no cause for alarm. The child is just acting out a dream. Accidents are rare, but it is obviously wise to make sure that the bottom windows of a child's room are always securely fastened.

Adequate rest, nourishing food, and plenty of exercise go a long way toward keeping your children fit and well and safe from infection. But you will go one important step further in guarding your children's health if you make sure that they have regular checkups with the doctor. Through such visits, the doctor will be able to chart your child's progress and see that he is protected against certain diseases by immunization, as well as detecting any health

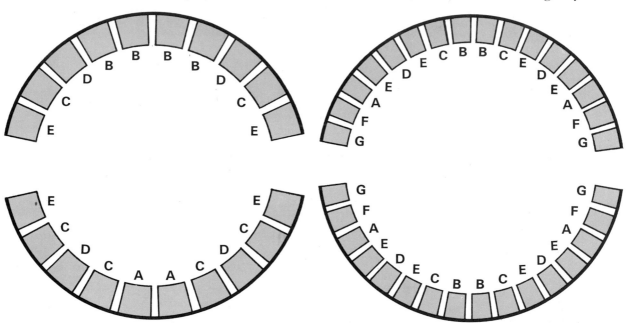

First teeth

A 5-10 months
B 8-12 months
C 12-14 months
D 16-22 months
E 24-30 months

The age at which a child's first and permanent teeth comes through varies, but teeth usually appear in the same order (generally in pairs or groups) as shown by the lettering on this diagram. The average child will have his full set of 20 baby teeth by the age of 2½, and these will have been replaced by adult teeth by the time he is 14. The final four "wisdom teeth" come later, and some children never develop them at all.

Second teeth

A 5-7 years
B 6-8 years
C 7-9 years
D 9-11 years
E 10-12 years
F 11-13 years
G 16-21 years

Above: sugary snacks spell danger to healthy teeth. Sugar helps form the acid that causes cavities.

Left: twice-a-day toothbrushing should begin as soon as a toddler's first teeth are all through.

problem early, when it stands the very best chance of being treated successfully.

How often should a child have a checkup? The answer depends on his age. During the first year, a baby should be seen by the doctor about once a month. Toddlers will probably need about three medical examinations a year, but these are generally reduced to two during the preschool period. While in school, your child should be examined regularly once a year by the family physician or a pediatrician.

Your doctor will advise you about the details of immunization (see schedule on page 34), which will probably require additional trips to the doctor's office. Make sure you keep a careful record of each shot and the date on which it was given. You will need this information when your child starts school or goes to camp, or if you should move and change your doctor.

Preschoolers may be upset by vaccinations

and by physical examinations in general. You will help your child best by remaining calm yourself, and holding him, or staying within sight, while the doctor treats him. By the time the child is three, he is less likely to be alarmed if you tell him in advance what the doctor is going to do. But if he still gets frightened, continue to comfort him, rather than trying to tease him out of his fears.

Another important expedition for which you should prepare your child is his first visit to the dentist. When the child is about $2\frac{1}{2}$, it is a good idea to take him with you when you are going for a routine dental checkup, and let him stay with you while you are having treatment. On his next visit, around the age of three, he can have a simple inspection of his own teeth.

Although only baby teeth are visible for the first five years or so of a child's life, his 32 adult teeth have been forming in his jaw since just after he was born, and they will be almost complete by the time he goes to school. These teeth, which will have to serve for a lifetime, are built up from whatever nourishment the child receives during his early years—yet another reason why a child should be eating lots of milk, vegetables and fruit, and not too many sugars and sweets.

The demon sugar is once again the culprit when it comes to tooth decay. Sugar combines with bacteria in the mouth to produce the acid that causes cavities. And, although it is estimated that fluoride in drinking water can cut the number of cavities in children's teeth by two-thirds, experiments have shown that the fewest cavities of all occur among children who eat few sweetened foods. No amount of fluoride can make up for a poor diet.

Decayed and uncared-for teeth not only add to your dental bills, but can spoil your child's appearance. So help your children to develop healthy teeth by taking care over their diet and getting them to brush their teeth regularly two or three times a day, after meals, and especially before going to bed. This will probably mean endless reminders from you all the time your children are growing up, but you will find it easier if you start your child off with the idea that tooth-cleaning can be fun. If a toddler sees Mom and Dad brushing their teeth, it probably won't be long before he wants to try it too. An electric toothbrush may also help because it seems like a toy. And it is a good idea to keep a spare toothbrush and paste in the kitchen for use after meals. If you are fighting a losing battle, however, concentrate on night-time brushing and try to end your child's meals with a toothcleaning food, like a hard fruit or raw carrot. If your child likes chewing gum, make sure he gets the sugarless kind, which will be easier on his teeth.

A toddler can begin toothbrushing when he has a full set of 20 baby teeth, around the age of $2\frac{1}{2}$ or 3. Care of these teeth is important, because if they are lost through decay, the child's second teeth will not have sufficient space to grow through properly. So once your child has started going to the dentist, make sure he gets a regular checkup twice a year.

Your care during his early years will give your child the best possible start toward a healthy life. But, as he leaves behind the busy, worrisome, and exciting years of childhood, you are bound to look a little apprehensively toward the years that lie ahead—years that will bring new challenges, for you and your child, as he steps out of childhood and on into the turbulent phase of adolescence.

Teens Without Tears

3

During adolescence the teenager has to cope with physical and emotional changes that can make it hard for him even to understand himself. Parents may find a moody teenager trying, but it is their continued love and support that will see him safely through this important stage

"Promiscuity among teenagers soaring, says doctor." "Parents didn't know their son was a junkie." "10 wounded in student riots." Headlines like these are enough to alarm any parent of a teenager today. And even serious books on teenagers may offer little comfort. All too often, they make adolescence sound like a dreadful disease that takes hold of a normal, happy youngster and transforms him overnight into an alien being with whom communication is impossible.

Of course, everyone knows that the teenage years are a critical period. Teenagers are undergoing tremendous physical and emotional changes. Adolescence, however, does not change the character of your child, and it need not destroy happy family relationships. It is simply another special stage in your special child's path to growth, and by understanding what is happening to your teenager, you can help him pass through this stage with the minimum of growing pains. For your child needs you now as much as ever—despite any appearances to the contrary—and with your continued love and guidance, his teenage years will not prove too much for either of you to handle.

Your child won't explode into adolescence overnight. The changes that lead to puberty are gradual, starting around age 11 for girls and 13 for boys. They may begin a couple of years earlier or several years later. Thus, biologically speaking, a child may become a teenager as early as age 9 or as late as age 16, and his teenage years will span the whole period from these first stirrings of puberty to the age when he is mature enough to leave home and take up a life of his own.

What are the changes that transform a child

Increasingly aware of the world outside, the teenager needs to discuss, question, and try out the possibilities that life is beginning to offer, along with companions of his own age. The group is a useful bridge between family life and greater independence, and younger teenagers may enjoy organized group activities like scouting. Others may prefer a more flexible group of schoolfriends. Almost all teenagers love the shared excitement of a pop concert, and hero worship of a pop star is a normal phase in their developing relationships with the opposite sex. Rebellion is in the air, too, for teenagers often reject established ways of living and behaving.

into a teenager? For a girl, the arrival of puberty is, of course, marked by her first menstrual period. This will probably happen around her twelfth birthday, although it is perfectly normal for a girl to have her first period as early as age 9 or as late as 16.

Well before her first period, however, the hormones responsible for puberty will have brought about other changes in a young girl's body. A year or two before menstruation, she will put on several inches in height, develop feminine curves, and start to grow pubic hair. When you notice these changes in your daughter, it is time to prepare her for the onset of menstruation if you have not already done so. You should explain simply but accurately why periods happen, pointing out that they are a normal, healthy part of growing up into womanhood. It is important, too, to discuss openly any feelings your daughter may have about the changes in her body, and her growing interest in boys, and to give honest answers to her questions about the functioning of a boy's body, too.

A girl's first periods are likely to be irregular. It usually takes about three years for the menstrual cycle to settle down to a regular pattern, and, even then, the typical monthly cycle of a young girl is generally longer than that of an adult woman. Variations in a girl's individual menstrual timing are perfectly normal, and it is important to reassure your daughter on this point.

Puberty generally comes earlier for girls than for boys, but a boy may hit this phase in his development at any time between the ages of 10 and 16. For him, the first sign of puberty is an enlargement of the penis, testicles, and scrotum (the sac containing the testicles). Hair will start to sprout on his face and other parts of his body, and his voice will "break" and start to gradually deepen. Unlike girls, however, who have finished most of their growing before their first period, a boy will usually get taller after his sexual maturation, rather than before.

About midway in this period of bodily development—usually around age 14—a boy will experience his first ejaculation. It is import-

43

ant to explain to him, in advance, that he will have seminal emissions (wet dreams), and that these are a perfectly natural result of the accumulation of sperm and seminal fluid in his body. As with your daughter, your son should be told the facts about his own growth and developing interest in sex, and about the growth and feelings of girls.

Because the age of puberty is so variable, even two children who have kept pace with each other throughout childhood may branch off along different paths of physical development as they enter their teens. Thirteen-year-old Jerry may quickly shoot up to 5'9", while his pal Andrew sticks for a couple of years at pre-teen size before growing into a six-footer. Sandra may be displaying already prominent breasts by the age of 11, whereas her best friend Sue hasn't the faintest suspicion of a bump. Such differences can cause the early or late developer to feel miserably out of step with his friends. It is vital, therefore, for parents to realize that such variations are normal, to greet Sandra's new-found curves with pleasure, and to reassure Andrew that he is not going to be permanently dwarfed by his friends.

Much to the disgust of at least 80 per cent of adolescents, this period is also marked by that scourge of the teenage skin known as acne. This is directly caused by the hormones that bring about sexual changes, but it will be of little comfort to your teenager to tell him that acne is a sign of his growing maturity, that eunuchs do not suffer from acne, that acne never killed anyone, or that he will "grow out of it". Time probably will take care of acne, but it may not take care of the damage acne can do to a teenager's self-esteem.

A severe, or persistent, case of acne should be handled by a dermatologist. Over-the-counter acne "cures" are unlikely to bring more than temporary respite, and may not work at all. Each teenager is different, and a remedy that is all right for one may be all wrong for another. It is far better, therefore, to get a doctor's prescription for medication to meet the specific needs of your acne-sufferer.

With or without medication to back it up,

Far left: fashions in figures have changed over the centuries. When Rubens painted this full-breasted, heavy-hipped lady in the 1600's, those generous curves were considered very enticing.

Left: it's no comfort to today's teenager to know that fat was once beautiful. The modern ideal of a slender figure can make an overweight girl painfully conscious of her excess inches.

however, the best treatment for acne is careful cleansing and attention to diet. The skin should be kept free of excess grease by washing with hot water, soap, and a rough Turkish cloth, three or four times a day. And teenagers should be discouraged from squeezing blackheads or pimples—this will spread infection and may result in deep-pitted scars. They should also steer clear of the foods that may aggravate acne, such as sweets, starches, nuts, carbonated drinks, and fried or fatty foods.

Of course, these are the very foods that all teenagers should be avoiding as much as possible, because of their continuing need for a healthily-balanced diet to help them grow. Unfortunately, however, a recent survey has shown that 40 per cent of teenage boys and 60 per cent of teenage girls subsist on diets that cannot possibly meet their nutritional needs. Most of these young people skip breakfast and fill up for the rest of the day on junk foods.

A teenager needs the same healthy diet as a younger child (see page 28), with one exception—he needs *more* nourishment. The phenomenal rate of growth and change at puberty pushes food needs higher than at any other time in life, including pregnancy. And appetite keeps pace with the need. Teenagers often seem able to eat their way through unbelievably large amounts of food and still go on to raid the fridge for more. This is fine, so long as a mother keeps a fair balance between health-building and starchy foods at mealtimes and stocks her fridge with plenty of nutritious extras. Remember, the more nourishing food you give your teenager at home, the less likely he is to spend on snacks.

If your teenager is a confirmed breakfast

skipper, try at least to thrust a glass of fruit juice and a slice of wholegrain toast and butter, or an apple, into his hand before he rushes off. And make sure you boost the meat, milk (or cheese), vegetable and fruit content of the meals he does eat at home. In addition, girls have a special need for extra iron once they have started their periods. Liver, meat, shellfish, and egg yolk are good sources for this, but a peanut butter sandwich or a couple of hamburgers a day can fill the bill equally well.

Alas, behind the teenager's increased appetite lurks the ogre of excess weight gain. For if appetite and food consumption continue at a high level beyond the phase of need, "puppy fat" can all too easily set in. This is particularly likely in girls for whom the growth phase is shorter. For the self-conscious adolescent fatty, excess weight is torture. And it is important to start the same treatment as for the plump young child (see page 32), with lots of affection and encouragement from you and a reduction of fattening foods until the youngster breaks the habit of eating more than she now needs. If this gets you nowhere, you should consult your doctor for a special diet. Above all, do not let your teenager—boy or girl—embark on any radical weight reduction program without first seeking the advice of a doctor. A crash diet could deprive him of the nutrition he needs for health.

Exercise is an important part of weight control and all-round fitness during the teenage years. Regular daily exercise burns up calories, develops strong muscles, improves the functioning of heart and lungs, and also helps a teenager to cope more effectively with the stresses and tensions of young adult life. Swimming, skating, tennis, fencing, running, or even rapid walking, are all excellent exercise for a teenager. It is important, however, to see that your son or daughter does not "overdo it" and injure his health in an eagerness to win at competitive sports or to build a broader or more shapely body.

Far more likely, however, is that your teenager will not be interested in exercise at all. Topping a recent poll of teenage hobbies were movies, reading, and going out with the gang.

Exercise is vital for healthy muscular development during the teenage years when a young person's body is still growing. Energetic sports and games give teenagers an opportunity to express the urge for excitement and hardy adventure that is part of their deep need for independence, and exercise of all kinds can provide a valuable outlet for some of the stresses of young adult life.

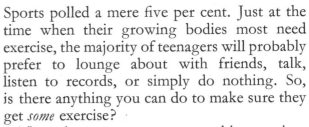

Sports polled a mere five per cent. Just at the time when their growing bodies most need exercise, the majority of teenagers will probably prefer to lounge about with friends, talk, listen to records, or simply do nothing. So, is there anything you can do to make sure they get *some* exercise?

There is no easy answer to this question. Doctors point out that the best time to solve the problem was at least five years ago, for a child who got interested in sport then is likely to stay active in his teens. But if you have a lazy teenager on your hands now, you could try pointing out the benefits of exercise in terms of looking good, or as a way to combat some of the ills of modern living. Encourage him to walk to school if you can, and get Dad to be firm about not lending him the car too often. And, if nothing else, be thankful if Michael or Mary wants to spend the evening dancing at a discotheque. That's good exercise too.

It may also be comforting to know that periods of lethargy are a natural part of growing up, when so much energy is needed for growth and development, for rebelling against authority, and for anxious self-

questioning. Agreed, such bouts of torpor can be infuriating to busy parents. Your teenager may be hard to wake in the mornings, prefer to stay in bed till noon, or spend the day mooning about the house, or brooding in his room. He may refuse to wash or pick up the clothes he has left strewn·about, and complain regularly that he "couldn't care less" about anything. Yet, although he seems stricken with day-long lassitude, he will insist on staying up late as a sign of independence.

How does a mother cope with all this? Well, it helps to understand that the physical and emotional changes with which your child is grappling right now are far more bewildering to him than they are to you. He feels lonely, unable to understand himself, and convinced that no one else can possibly know how he feels. It may test your patience to the limit, but this is a time when you and your husband must help and guide, support and comfort, be calm and uncritical—without being patronizing. Bitter arguments can make the child who is no longer a child feel lonelier still on his uncomfortable perch between childhood and adulthood.

A teenager needs plenty of sleep, but nightly feuds over bedtimes are likely to leave him more determined than ever to be independent, and you more exhausted than he is. With a newly-fledged teenager, it is best to discuss bedtimes, to be ready to give or take an hour or so, and try to arrive at some compromise. You may find it easier to allow, say, a couple of late nights a week—preferably on weekends— provided he goes to bed earlier on schooldays. With an older teenager, however, it is probably best to make a declaration of faith in his own judgment by letting him know that you trust him to make up his own mind about the right time to go to bed.

The same degree of flexibility should not apply, however, to times of coming home at night. And you should be strong enough to support your teenager with a firm "no" over any outings you consider unsuitable. Ten to one, your teenager will be like 15-year-old Georgina, who begged her parents to let her go to an all-night party, but was inwardly

relieved when they insisted she be home by 11.30. Secretly scared about what might happen if no one cared about where she was or when she came home, but not wanting to appear foolish in front of her friends, Georgina was able to save face by telling them that her dreary old parents wouldn't let her stay later.

In many ways, the teenager can be compared to the toddler. Like the young child, he is anxiously feeling his way toward independence, and exulting in the sense of power it brings, but at the same time needing to retreat to the safety of home base when some of the responsibilities of independence become too

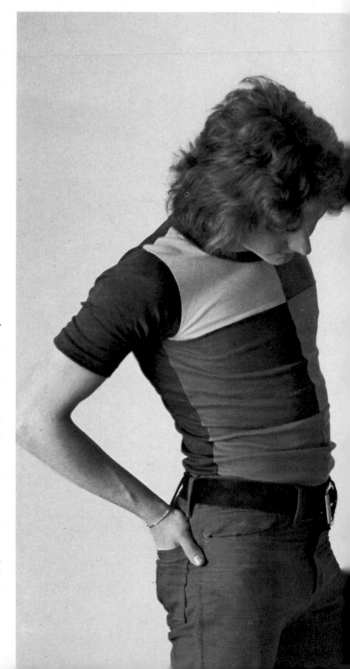

much to handle. Not that the teenager would ever admit this, of course—and not that the tactful parent would make it obvious. "The art of being a teenager's parent," as one doctor puts it, "lies in making yourself reasonably unobtrusive without abdicating responsibility prematurely or refusing altogether to accept the unglamorous but necessary role of a middle-aged square. If you aren't a bit square, your teenager will have nothing to rebel against."

Probably the one aspect of teenage rebellion that worries today's parents most is drug-taking. Statistics tell us that drug abuse is the major cause of death among young people. And doctors estimate that virtually all teenagers today will try drugs, or at least have the chance to try them.

If you cannot prevent your teenager from encountering drugs, how can you ensure that he doesn't take them? The first step is to know the facts about drugs yourself. If you make inaccurate statements, your child is not likely to place much faith in your judgment. The

The communication gap often seems to yawn far wider during adolescence. Parents won't help by being too critical of a youngster's changing attitudes, and need to listen to his views, too.

chart on this page will give you some of the information you need, and a good book on the subject is *Drugs, Parents, and Children* by Dr. Mitchell S. Rosenthal and Ira Mothner. It gives lots of helpful advice and suggestions for answering some of the tricky questions teenagers are likely to ask. The next step is to be ready and willing to discuss the issues openly and unemotionally with your son or daughter, whenever the subject of drugs comes up. And come up it will. Most teenagers today have strong feelings about drugs and even those who have never tried them will almost certainly defend to the death the right of their peers to do so. Don't panic, but let your child have his say, discuss his arguments, and make it obvious that your opinions are reasonable ones, based on knowledge, not prejudice.

While being aware of the facts about drugs, you should try not to be constantly on the

Drug-taking is an issue of vital concern to every parent of a teenager today. A youngster will be far more willing to accept his parents' guidance on this subject if they are willing to discuss the issues openly and obviously have a sound knowledge of the facts to back up their attitudes. In this chart you will find some of the basic information all parents should know about the most commonly used drugs, their uses, and effects.

Drugs

Type of drug	PSYCHEDELICS		STIMULANTS
	Cannabis	Hallucinogens	Amphetamines
Names	Marijuana, Hashish	LSD, Mescaline, Psilocybin, Scopolamine, STP	Benzedrine, Dexedrine, Desoxyn, Methadrine, Preludin, Several other types
Slang names	Pot, hash, grass, weed, tea, kif, Mary Jane, reefer, joint	Acid, cube, tab, blue cheer, sunshine, white lightning	A, speed, pep pills, ups, co-pilots, crystal bennies, meth, dex
How taken	Inhaled or swallowed	Swallowed, usually on sugar	Usually swallowed, may be injected
Short-term effects	Clinging smell of burning grass, Relaxation, breakdown of inhibitions, alteration of perception, laughter without reason, flushing.	Increased awareness, perceptual changes, increased energy, hallucinations and delusions, panic. Panic state may sometimes provoke severe recurrent mental disturbance.	Elation, talkativeness, restlessness, jerky movements, dilated pupils, rapid pulse, flushing, decreased appetite, lack of fatigue.
Effects of habitual use	Often none. Feeling of indifference, fatigue, lethargy.	Possibly none. Poor concentration, work deteriorates, possibly increased delusions & panic. Can produce permanent mental disturbance.	Alternating elation and aggression, irritability with depression, poor appetite & weight loss, looks exhausted but can't sleep. Delusions with large doses. Development of dependence on drug.

50

look-out for signs that your youngster is misusing drugs. Apparent evidence can all too easily be confused with the natural "ups and downs" of adolescence—abrupt swings of mood, dreaminess, secretiveness, irritability, or restlessness, for example. And most importantly, adolescents need to feel that their parents trust them and that they can trust their parents. If they think you are "spying," they will react with hostility and you won't be able to help. If they feel you are expecting them to be using drugs, they may well react by doing just that—and blaming you for it afterwards. Provided you know your youngster well, you will probably be able to spot any unusual changes in his behavior without having to rifle his room for drugs.

What if you do discover that your teenager is using drugs? British psychiatrist Alexander Mitchell has noted that parents usually react to this discovery in one of the following ways. They are shocked and unbelieving, numb and hopeless, resentful, quick to blame others for the problem, or reject their child altogether. All of these very human reactions, says Dr. Mitchell, provoke equally emotional counter-responses in the adolescent, and parents and child find themselves caught in a blind alley of hostility and aggression.

It is far wiser not to confront your child at the moment of discovery, but to allow a cooling-off period before discussing the problem as calmly as you can, and letting him present his side. Try to keep a sense of perspective, and take an honest look at why, and how seriously, your child has been experimenting with drugs. Finally, make sure you know where to turn for help—and turn to It If your child's drug problem is obviously too much for you to handle alone. Check out the

		DEPRESSANTS			
Cocaine	Nicotine	Alcohol	Barbiturates	Narcotics	Tranquilizers
	Cigarettes, Cigars, Pipe, Snuff	Beer, Distilled spirits, Wine	Amytal, Chloral hydrate, Doriden, Nembutal, Phenobarbital, Seconal	Heroin, Morphine, Opium, Methadone, Percodan, Codeine, Demerol	Librium, Miltown/Equanil, Thorazine & many others
C, Coke			Sleepers, downers, goof balls, yellow jackets, red devils	H, horse, junk, shit, smack, stuff, snow, crap, garbage, O, hop	
Sniffed or injected	Inhaled or sniffed	Swallowed	Swallowed	Injected, sniffed or swallowed	Swallowed
Feeling of self-confidence and power, intense exhilaration.	Relaxation, constriction of blood vessels.	Relaxation, breakdown of inhibitions, decreased alertness, euphoria, depression, slurred speech, impaired coordination, nausea, unconsciousness, hangover.	Relaxation, euphoria, drowsiness, impaired coordination and judgement, slurred speech, appears dull as though sleepwalking.	Relaxation, euphoria, hallucinations, slurred speech, poor coordination, decreased alertness, may vomit, pupils very small, injection mark.	Relaxation, lessening of inhibitions, relief of anxiety and tension, drowsiness, blurred vision. Lack of coordination with large doses.
Irritability, depression, psychosis. Development of dependence on drug.	Headache, loss of appetite, nausea, impaired breathing. Development of dependence on drug.	Prolonged heavy use can lead to malnutrition, temporary impotence, social deterioration, psychosis, delerium tremens ulcers, liver & brain damage. Development of dependence on drug.	Irritability, excessive drowsiness, poor concentration, confusion, slurred speech and staggering. Development of dependence on drug.	Rapidly varying moods of elation & depression, loss of appetite and weight, constipation, temporary impotence, lethargy, self-neglect. Rapid development of dependence on drug.	Persistent drowsiness & poor concentration. Development of dependence on drug.

resources available in your community—schools, churches, mental health clinics, hospitals, private social agencies, or self-help groups that organize drug-counselling for the young—or consult your own family doctor.

It is important, however, for parents to keep their heads over the whole question of teenagers and drugs. Adolescents are persons in their own right, and must eventually decide for themselves whether or not to use drugs. If parents respect the individuality of their child and are ready to support and advise, without bullying, the teenager is likely to dismiss drugs as not for him, even if he has sampled them once or twice out of sheer curiosity. The teenager who misuses drugs has deeper emotional problems that would have manifested themselves in other ways had drugs not been available. So parents should not focus their attention only on the drugs, but on the reasons for the anxiety, loneliness, frustration, or whatever, that may be causing the young person to seek escape through drugs.

In comparison with drug-taking, smoking and drinking may seem far less of a problem. But cigarettes and alcohol are also drugs. Seventy per cent of 15-year-olds smoke, and consumption of alcohol in this age-group is rising. Unfortunately, warnings about the links between smoking and cancer are not likely to carry much weight with a teenager who has been raised under the threat of nuclear disaster and worldwide pollution, and for whom the age of 40 seems light years away. Of course, you should tell your teenager the facts about cigarette addiction, but bear in mind that he will probably be far more impressed by the fact that his friends won't like his bad breath, that smoking stains the teeth yellow, and that it will slow him down at sports.

The dangers of alcohol will almost certainly have come up during talks with your teenager about other drugs. Again, you have to know the facts and be consistent in your attitudes. Surveys have shown that the teenagers who misuse alcohol are usually those whose parents have mixed feelings about drinking or who drink heavily themselves but forbid their children to drink until they are 21. Dr. Morris

E. Chafetz, head of the National Institute on Alcohol Abuse and Alcoholism, suggests that problems might be prevented if children learned to drink wisely in a social setting at home. So, if you do have alcohol in your home, it seems advisable to allow your youngster a little beer or wine on special occasions, when you consider him old enough, rather than issuing a strict veto that may provoke him into sneaking off to drink with his friends.

One factor that may make your child's teenage years particularly trying for you is that you may be at a difficult phase in your own life. Your teenager is feeling insecure, but probably you have feelings of insecurity too, particularly if your life up to now has been centered exclusively around your home and family. As your children grow away, you may feel that you are losing your role as mother and have no other to take its place. That is why it is important to think about your own future even before your last child enters adolescence, to cultivate interests and friendships beyond the family, and to plan for, or take up, some absorbing work or activity outside the home.

It helps, too, to remember that the teenage years are not all problems. On the plus side of being a teenager's parent is the pleasure of being in close contact with the excitement of youth, of being able to share in the hopes, dreams, and challenges of a new generation. There is the occasional delight of going out in the company of a young adult, of seeing the world through his eyes, and of keeping your own ideas flexible through discussing so many aspects of life with a newly maturing mind. There is the joy of seeing your child gradually grow into a strong and healthy adult with a mind and a sense of responsibility of his own. And, before too many years are over, you will probably have the satisfaction of seeing your child set up a home of his own, knowing that it is your love and example that will help him, in turn, to raise his own family.

When a father and his teenage son can enjoy a common interest, they have a valuable opportunity to stay in touch with each other, and to go on appreciating each other's company all through life.

Looking After Your Husband

4

It's women and women's problems that are hitting the headlines today. And men are often blamed for those problems. But is it all that easy being a man? Men are having a harder time today than ever before. They're the ones who suffer most from the unprecedented stresses and strains of modern living. They're the ones most at risk from industrial hazards, from pollution, and from the strain of making life-and-death decisions on the road They're the ones who all too often drive themselves too hard to provide financial security for their families. They're the ones most at risk from heart disease, lung cancer, and ulcers. And they are the ones who die youngest. Today, the average women lives six to seven years longer than the average man.

No one knows for sure why men should be the losers when it comes to health. But one thing is certain. Men can live longer and healthier lives—and their wives can help them do it. A man's home life is known to be vital in helping him withstand the pressures and diseases of our modern world. Married men live longer and generally stay healthier than bachelors. So, how can a wife make the most of this advantage in ensuring that she and her husband have a happy, healthy, and long life—together?

The first important step is a regular medical checkup. Probably your husband will agree that this is a fine idea, but will keep putting it off. Men, says Dr. Solomon D. Klotz of Orlando, Florida, "hate to take time off from work, they feel it is unmanly to be sick, and much more so to be routinely checked. Men are always apologetic and embarrassed when facing a doctor under these circumstances. I often get the impression that the patient wishes he could show me a real honest-to-goodness illness."

Your husband might feel differently if he knew that even the most serious ills to which a man is prone can be effectively dealt with if they are detected early enough. Illness usually doesn't happen overnight. It is more often the result of processses that have been developing for years. A thorough checkup can reveal conditions that might lead to illness long before a man notices any symptoms himself—and while he still has time to clear it up. By detecting health problems before they become serious, periodic checkups can save years of emotional, physical, and financial strain. And then, of course, there is always the possibility that a health check may pronounce your husband 100 per cent fit—a marvellous boost to anyone's well-being.

How, then, do you get a busy man to take time out for a checkup? Sometimes the best way is to go right ahead and make an appointment for him. Choose a date far enough in advance not to clash with any of your husband's plans. And why not make arrangements to go along with him? After all, you should be having a regular checkup, too. Checkups for one, let alone two, may seem expensive, but the cost dwindles if you look at it in terms of preventing a possible stay in hospital, or of adding precious years to your life.

If you are reluctant to take up your doctor's time with a routine health check, you may prefer to make an appointment for your

Helping your husband to stay healthy means a happier life for all the family. For when Dad feels fighting fit, he not only gets more fun out of his life but he is more fun to have around the family, too.

Good health maintenance for your husband should include a regular medical checkup. Routine checks can pinpoint possible problems early and so give a man a personal plan for safeguarding his health.

Right: here are the kind of tests that will plot a head-to-toe profile of your husband's health.

Below: metal electrodes attached to chest and ankles test how well a man's heart is working.

husband at one of the special screening centers that exist in many major cities for this very purpose. There, he can undergo a whole battery of sophisticated tests that will plot a complete, head-to-toe profile of his health. Apart from physiological measurements, physical examinations, and laboratory tests, some such centers make use of computers to collect detailed information about every aspect of a man's life that may have a bearing on his health—facts about himself, his surroundings, his work, his home life, his heredity, and his entire medical history. Most men thoroughly enjoy telling the computer all about themselves, and find it a whole lot easier to give frank answers by pushing a button than by replying to a doctor or filling out a printed questionnaire.

Specialists in preventive medicine recommend that a man have his first checkup as early as age 25. But, provided all is well, a further check every two or three years until age 45 should be sufficient. Over 45's, however, are advised to have a medical examination at least once a year.

One of the commonest of all health problems revealed by a checkup is overweight, which is a major health hazard for a man. Doctors have calculated that, with every 10 per cent of weight he gains over the desirable weight for his height, a man risks cutting his life expectancy by 13 per cent. Even 10 or 15 pounds of extra weight make a man more vulnerable to most serious diseases. Heart disease, high blood pressure, and strokes, for example, are twice as common in people who are overweight. And there are plenty more grim statistics to show that all sorts of other disabling or fatal disorders are likely to go along with excess fat.

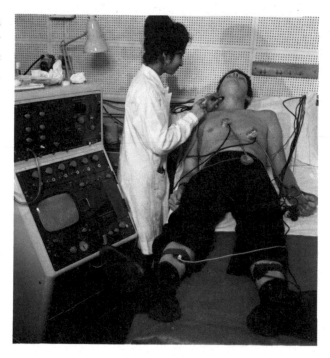

There is, however, one ray of light in this gloomy picture. A man can shed his excess pounds and put himself out of danger. No one is going to pretend that it is easy, but it can be done. And the best way of helping a man reduce is to share his efforts with him. If you and your husband are both trying to lose weight, you can make a game out of it, compare notes on your progress, and bolster each other's morale. But even if you don't need to slim, you can still be your man's best ally in the fight against fat, because you are the one who chooses the menus.

This doesn't mean that you have to switch overnight from generous helpings of potatoes and rich desserts to salads without dressing, or bananas and skim milk. Crash diets are good for no man—or woman. Not only may they fail to supply the body with enough essential

Your Husband's Checkup

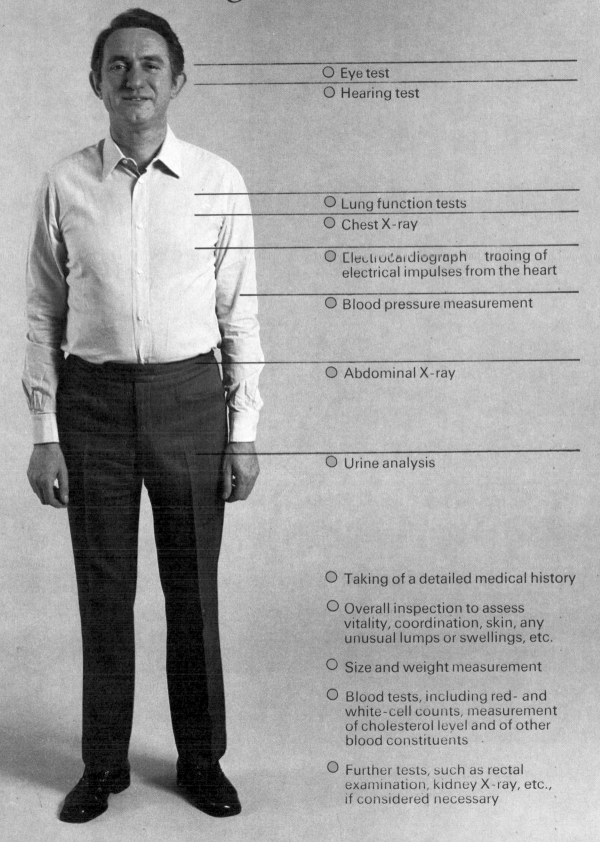

- ○ Eye test
- ○ Hearing test

- ○ Lung function tests
- ○ Chest X-ray
- ○ Electrocardiograph — tracing of electrical impulses from the heart
- ○ Blood pressure measurement
- ○ Abdominal X-ray
- ○ Urine analysis

- ○ Taking of a detailed medical history
- ○ Overall inspection to assess vitality, coordination, skin, any unusual lumps or swellings, etc.
- ○ Size and weight measurement
- ○ Blood tests, including red- and white-cell counts, measurement of cholesterol level and of other blood constituents
- ○ Further tests, such as rectal examination, kidney X-ray, etc., if considered necessary

nutrients for health, but they require super-human efforts of willpower to succeed. Few people can keep to such diets for long, and weight that is lost in a hurry will come right back on again when dieting stops. "On-and-off" dieting like this, say doctors, can actually be more harmful than being continuously over-weight. Successful dieting, on the other hand, means gradually introducing new eating habits that are easy to continue even when the excess pounds have gone.

Little by little, you can replace fattening foods by equally delicious substitutes that will satisfy your husband's appetite without putting on extra weight. Lean steaks, pot roasts, hamburgers, lamb and veal chops, chicken and turkey, for example, are all high in protein but low in fattening power. So choose these meats a lot more often than bacon, pork, sausages, or ham, and switch to fish every once in a while. Broiled or baked foods have fewer calories than fried ones. And how about serving an extra green vegetable instead of potatoes, pasta, or rice? Fresh fruit with plain yoghurt could stand in for ice cream or pies. Stewed fruit for breakfast can taste just as good as cereal. Try substituting cottage cheese or meat spreads for cream cheese, jam, or honey, and celery or fruit for crackers. You may also like to use non-fat powdered milk in coffee or tea, or a squeeze of lemon and a pinch of salt instead of butter on vegetables.

Once you have got the idea, you can work out many more variations for yourself. A calorie chart in the kitchen and a low-calorie cookbook will help you here. It may seem a nuisance to have to count calories, but remember those wretched health statistics and stick to your guns. If your husband is in on the act, enlist his help for the calculations. Then he may remember something about calories when he eats away from home, too. Try serving just enough food to satisfy your husband's appetite, and keep leftovers well out of sight. Taking second helpings can often be just a habit. It may also help to serve meals on smaller plates—that way they will look bigger. Regular meals are best, but try not to have your last meal too close to bedtime. Since little food is needed for energy while you are asleep, most of it will be converted into fat while you slumber away unawares.

Quite apart from slimming, many women worry about the amount of fat in their husband's diet because of suspected links between cholesterol and heart disease. Cholesterol is a material that is derived from animal fats in food and that is also manufactured by the body. A certain amount of cholesterol is essential to health—it forms two per cent of the

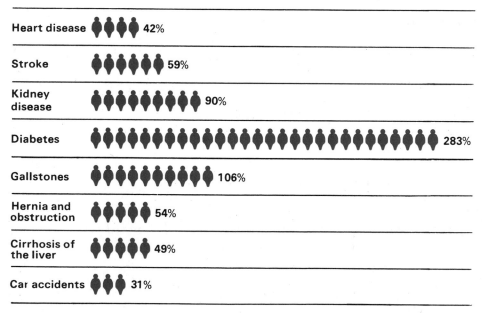

Heart disease	42%
Stroke	59%
Kidney disease	90%
Diabetes	283%
Gallstones	106%
Hernia and obstruction	54%
Cirrhosis of the liver	49%
Car accidents	31%

Right: this fellow once surely took the prize for heavyweight husbands. An 18th-century jail keeper called Daniel Lambert, he tipped the scales at 738½ pounds. Left: it really isn't fun to be fat. In fact, fat can be fatal, as these statistics prove. They show how overweight people run much more danger of dying from certain causes than people of normal weight—each symbol representing 10 per cent of increased risk. The only crumb of comfort statisticians can offer the fatties is their low suicide rate: 25 per cent less than average.

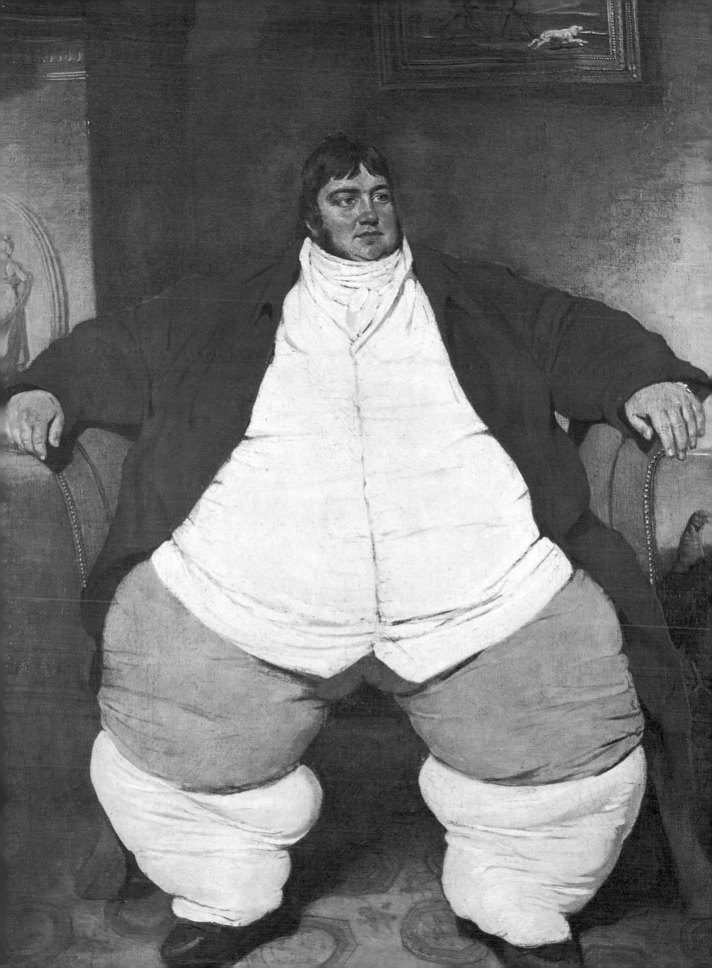

How much should a man weigh? Check this table to find out. It shows, not average weights for men of different builds, but *desirable* weights—the ones that go with better health and longer life. Calculated with indoor clothing and shoes on, they apply to any man over the age of 25, meaning that, ideally, a man should not gain any extra pounds over the years. Frame sizes vary, of course, so the chart should only be used as a guide. But it can provide a useful target weight for a man to aim at, and may give good reason to ponder as he tucks into his next hearty, and unnecessary, snack.

Ideal Weights

MEN OF AGES 25 AND OVER			
Height Feet Ins	Small Frame	Medium Frame	Large Frame
5 2	112–120	118–129	126–141
5 3	115–123	121–133	129–144
5 4	118–126	124–136	132–148
5 5	121–129	127–139	135–152
5 6	124–133	130–143	138–156
5 7	128–137	134–147	142–161
5 8	132–141	138–152	147–166
5 9	136–145	142–156	151–170
5 10	140–150	146–160	155–174
5 11	144–154	150–165	159–179
6 0	148–158	154–170	164–184
6 1	152–162	158–175	168–189
6 2	156–167	162–180	173–194
6 3	160–171	167–185	178–199
6 4	164–175	172–190	182–204

weight of the brain, for example—but too much cholesterol builds up in the arteries and may play a part in causing coronary disease or stroke. So, although the case against cholesterol has not been proved, most doctors advise moderating the animal fat content of our diet as a wise precaution. And this applies to lean men as well as plump ones.

Cholesterol-rich foods include fat meats, pork, sausages, egg yolk, butter, cheese, pastry, cream, meat drippings, and other animal fats. So it is wise to avoid too many of these foods and to trim away the visible fat from your meat. Since eating vegetable fats will actually reduce the amount of cholesterol in the blood, try to include in your diet some vegetable oils (such as corn, sunflower, and olive oil), fish oils, or polyunsaturated margarines.

While a certain amount of fat is essential for any man's health, two foods should definitely be cut right down for a man who wants to slim. These are sugar and alcohol. Sugar supplies nothing but energy, and when it is not used for energy, it is laid down as fat. What's more, some doctors are convinced that there is a link between high sugar consumption and heart disease. As for alcohol, this is nearly twice as fattening, weight for weight, as sugar. And it has the double disadvantage of stimulating appetite. Ideally, alcohol should be out for a man who is slimming. If that seems impossible, you might decide to try and cut out more calories from other foods to compensate for the occasional drink (see page 64). But it is not wise to do this regularly lest a man go short of some important food element in the process— quite apart from feeling hungrier and weakening in his resolve to diet.

Any diet should, of course, be combined with regular exercise. For, although exercise alone cannot reduce excess weight—it would take a 35-mile walk or 100 holes of golf to get rid of just one pound of fat—exercise is just as important as diet in weight control. Only when eating and exercise go hand in hand can a man reach a desirable weight and stay there.

Exercise is not just important for the dieter. It is vital for any man's health, be he fat or lean. Exercise can make a man look, think, sleep, and feel better. It can help release pent-up tension and stress, prevent aches and pains, improve his circulation, and keep his heart and lungs in good shape.

The key to safe and effective exercise, say doctors, is to introduce a little bit of action into every day. Sudden bouts of strenuous exercise can be dangerous because the body just isn't

prepared for the strain. A man who leads a sedentary life needs an activity that starts out gently but can become gradually more demanding as he gets fitter. And it needs to be something he can fit into his daily routine.

So what sort of exercise should your husband take? And how can you get him to take it? One of the best and easiest forms of exercise that will fit into anyone's daily routine is walking. Maybe you could persuade your husband to walk to work or the station. It will probably help if you can walk along part of the way with him. Or, if the children don't need to be supervised, how about a walk before bed—this will also help you sleep better. And exercise after meals is particularly good, because more food is burned up faster just after eating.

If your husband is interested in sports, so much the better. Swimming, running, skating, skiing, tennis, squash, table tennis, or bicycling are all excellent activities that you could share. Golf is good, too, and so is jogging, provided your husband gets a doctor's approval first. Or how about setting up your own exercise program at home? The Royal Candian Air Force 11-minute a day exercise plan is a good one that you could both try. Alternatively, you may be able to persuade your husband to join a physical fitness group. More and more of these groups are being formed nowadays for both sexes. If your community doesn't have one, why not try getting a few friends together and start the ball rolling?

One of the important hidden bonuses of exercise is that it can help a man to give up smoking. And there can be few people around today who are not aware of at least some of the dangers of this habit. It is bad enough to know that a smoker runs 20 times the normal risk of dying of lung cancer, and three times the risk of heart disease or stroke. But experts have now calculated that a man over 25 who smokes a pack or more cigarettes a day is likely to lose $6\frac{1}{4}$ years of his estimated life. Two or more packs a day can lose a man $8\frac{1}{4}$ years of life—about six minutes for every cigarette that he smokes.

Maybe your husband feels it is not worth giving up cigarettes at this stage, because any damage to his health is already done. Studies have shown, however, that damaged lung tissue will heal itself once smoking stops. Even for heavy smokers, the risk of lung cancer steadily decreases with each year after giving up smoking, and the odds against getting any other cigarette-linked diseases improve immediately cigarettes are given up.

One thing that won't help, however, is switching to cigars or a pipe, or choosing cigarettes with a low tar and nicotine content. Unlike most regular pipe or cigar-smokers, a man who has been used to cigarettes will almost certainly inhale the smoke from pipe or cigar and take just as many harmful substances down into his lungs as if he continued with cigarettes. As for switching to low tar and nicotine cigarettes, this ignores another potential health hazard in cigarettes—sugar. Recent research has indicated that cigarettes with a high sugar content may increase the risk of lung disease, even if their tar and nicotine levels are low. Low-sugar cigarettes, on the other hand, tend to be high in tar and nicotine. So the smoker can't win. As doctors say, the only safe bet is to give up smoking.

How can you help your husband to break the smoking habit? If you smoke, too, it is wise to try quitting or cutting down with him. If you don't smoke, how about sharing his ordeal by cutting down on something you are particularly fond of—candies or sweet desserts, for example. Put the money you save aside and spend it on an outing for two. Or how about using it for those medical checkups?

This makes it sound as if giving up smoking were easy, and of course it isn't. Whether a man cuts down gradually or quits abruptly, it takes a lot of willpower. Drugs from the doctor may help, and so may chewing gum (the sugarless kind), nibbling fresh fruit, sipping glasses of water, having a mouthwash after a meal, or keeping an unlighted cigarette in the mouth. It is a good idea for a man to try quitting when there is a major break in his normal routine—during a vacation, or after an illness or operation, for example. Changes in routine during the cutting-down period can also help, and so can riding in "no smoking" railroad cars and going to places where smoking is forbidden. A booklet to get is "If You Want to Give Up Cigarettes" published by the American Cancer Society. It is packed with invaluable ideas and advice for the would-be nonsmoker—and his wife.

One of the reasons why many men start smoking in the first place, of course, is in an effort to cope with stress. A certain amount of stress is part and parcel of living. Joy, for example, is just as much of a stress as anger. Watching a football game on TV is stressful, and so is any sudden excitement. All these emotions cause chemicals to be released into the system to help the body cope with the extra claims being made on it. Normally, once the stress is over, the effect of

Calories--In and Out

To lose weight, a man must eat less or exercise more, preferably both. This chart shows you the number of calories in certain foods and the time, in *minutes*, that it would take for various activities to burn them up. For example, a man would have to sleep for 300 minutes, or 5 hours, to burn up the 350 calories in a hamburger—or bowl for 80 minutes. It may seem to take a lot of activity to use up those calories, but the effects of exercise do build up in time. If food intake stays the same, just two extra brisk half-hour walks a day could add up to 20 lost pounds in a year.

Food	Calories per Serving	Sleeping	Walking	Bowling	Golf	Tennis	Bicycling	Swimming	Running
Raw carrot	42	36	8	10	8	6	5	4	2
Boiled egg	77	66	15	17	15	11	9	7	4
Fried egg	110	94	21	25	22	15	13	10	6
Bread/butter	78	67	15	18	16	11	10	7	4
Bacon (two strips)	96	82	18	22	19	14	12	9	5
Apple (large)	101	87	19	23	20	14	12	9	5
Beer (glass)	114	98	22	26	23	16	14	10	6
Orange juice (glass)	120	103	23	27	24	17	15	11	6
Milk (glass)	166	142	32	38	33	23	20	15	9
Pancake/syrup	124	106	24	28	25	17	15	11	6
Cheese pizza	180	154	35	41	36	25	22	16	9
½ breast, fried chicken	232	199	45	53	46	33	28	21	12
T-bone steak	235	201	45	53	47	33	29	21	12
Hamburger	350	300	67	80	70	49	43	31	18
Tuna fish salad sandwich	278	238	53	63	56	39	34	25	14
Ice cream soda	255	219	49	58	51	36	31	23	13
1/6 apple pie	377	323	73	86	75	53	46	34	19
Spaghetti	396	339	76	90	79	56	48	35	20
Strawberry shortcake	400	343	77	91	80	56	49	36	21

What's in a Drink?

Alcohol is a major enemy for weight-watchers, adding on extra inches much faster than food. Take a look at what each of these drinks represents in terms of food, and you may be surprised at how much your husband is eating when he drinks! That one cocktail, for example, counts for 150 calories—the equivalent in fattening power of one whole one-pound lobster. Details of the drinks pictured and their calorie content appear below, with a few more of their approximate food equivalents. The calorie values are for the amount of drink in one glass or jigger. Any soda, tonic, or fruit juice will add on extra calories—about 10 to 15 a time.

As you will see, some drinks are less fattening than others. Dry wines and sherries, in particular, are less fattening than sweet ones, and red table wines usually have fewer calories than white.

1. Whiskey. One jigger = 120 calories.
That's equivalent to 40 cups of unsweetened coffee, or 8 Ritz crackers, or two medium-sized pancakes, or 4 tomatoes, or 4 cups of clear soup.

2. Wine. One wine glass = 100 calories.
That rates the same as 4 cups of green beans, or 6 teaspoons of sugar, or 2 heads of celery, or 2 strips of bacon, or an average serving of cereal.

3. Sherry. One sherry glass = 75 calories.
That counts as much as 7 medium cucumbers, or 3½ green peppers, or a cup of American grapes, or 4 large marshmallows, or one poached egg.

4. Beer. Eight ounces = 120 calories.
That is the equivalent of a Frankfurter, or a serving of shrimps, or two ounces of fried beef liver, or 2 oranges, or 1½ ounces of cheese.

5. Cocktail. One cocktail glass = 150 calories.
That rates as high as one whole 1 lb. lobster or 6 carrots, 1 serving of Apple Betty ,or 3 tablespoons of whipped cream, or 3 cups tomato juice.

6. Gin. One jigger = 115 calories.
That counts the same as 2 cups of strawberries, or 4½ cups of spinach, or 2 lettuces, or a grapefruit, or 1 slice of angelfood cake.

7. Brandy. One brandy glass = 80 calories.
That's equivalent to 3½ cups of mushrooms, or 1 cup of peas, or one ounce of hard candies, or 2 peaches, or 2 tablespoons of chocolate sauce.

1

these chemicals is neutralized. Trouble, however, comes when we undergo too much stress for too long. Unrelieved stress may then play its part in producing a host of physical and mental disturbances, from heart disease, high blood pressure, and ulcers, to headaches, indigestion, fatigue, anxiety and general feelings of depression.

Of course, we cannot cut stress entirely out of our own—or our husband's—lives. But any woman who feels that her husband's job is making too great and continued a demand on his health should seriously consider whether he might not be better off in a less stressful occupation. This may sound like a pretty drastic solution, but even being ready to discuss it as a possibility can do a lot to take the pressure off a man who feels that he must stick at a job that overtaxes him or make ever-increasing efforts to get ahead and earn more money for the sake of his family.

This is what happened to John. His job as an accountant with a small electrical firm suited him well enough until the company was taken over and he was promoted to a more responsible post. John found he was having to do twice as much work, and lived in fear of making an error that might cost him his job. "Several of my colleagues' jobs were eliminated after the takeover," says John, "And I was scared that I would be the next to go. With two boys in school and the house to pay for, I just couldn't afford to lose my job. I began to dread going to work. I would literally shake with fright all the way to the office. I tried to talk to my wife about it, but somehow she was always too busy to listen. I guess she just had too much to do, with the house and the kids, and all. In the end, I decided I'd have to see a doctor."

John's doctor was sympathetic. He prescribed tranquilizers and insisted that John take a couple of weeks off work. John and his wife managed to arrange for the children to stay with relatives and took a short vacation by themselves. "That was the greatest vacation I've ever spent," says John. "I felt so relaxed that I even forgot to take the tranquilizers. My wife and I were finally able to talk things over, and by the time we got back we'd decided

Cutting down those cigarettes is a sharp move for any wife to make. Smoking is a gamble with death, as this table shows. It demonstrates the risks that a smoker runs of dying within the next 10 years, according to his age and the number of cigarettes he smokes. Suppose, for example, that, for each 10 years of possible life, a man draws a ticket from a box containing one ticket marked "death" among a number of blanks. If he draws the marked ticket, he dies within 10 years. The figures in the table show the number of tickets among which the marked one is placed. Thus, for a non-smoker of 35, there is one marked ticket for the next 10 years in a box of 75, but for a heavy smoker of the same age, the ticket is one among 22. But remember, a man who gives up cigarettes can soon be up there with the same chances as someone who has never smoked.

what to do. I quit the firm and took a job with another small company in the country. And I'm sure the whole family is better for it."

John's job became "too much for him" because it was over-demanding. But some men may find their jobs stressful because they are unfulfilling and fail to make use of their special talents and skills. Derek, for example, hated his job as an insurance clerk. What he really wanted to do was to teach. And, with the help of his wife, and a good bit of scrimping and saving, that is what he did. Tom, on the other hand, was a clever draughtsman, who loved his work and was firm enough to refuse a promotion that would have taken him away from the drawing board—even though it meant staying at a lower salary.

All these men were able to opt for less stressful lives because they had the full backing of their wives. And it is important for a wife to let her husband know that she would far rather have him alive, well, and happy than suffering for the sake of a larger pay check. Of course, that is the way we all feel. It's just that husband and wife may get so caught up in the frantic scramble of money-earning and budgeting that they lose sight of the fact. Naturally a wife worries about having enough money to go around. And naturally parents want to give their children the best possible start in life. But provided a family has enough to eat, enough clothing, and a place to live, more money and more possessions will not add up to more happiness. A few luxuries are nice, but they

The Smoking Gamble

Age	Non-smokers	Smokers of: 1–14/day	15–24/day	25 or more/day
35–44	1 in 75	1 in 47	1 in 50	1 in 22
45–54	1 in 27	1 in 19	1 in 13	1 in 10
55–64	1 in 9	1 in 6	1 in 5	1 in 4
65–74	1 in 3	1 in 2	1 in 2	1 in 2

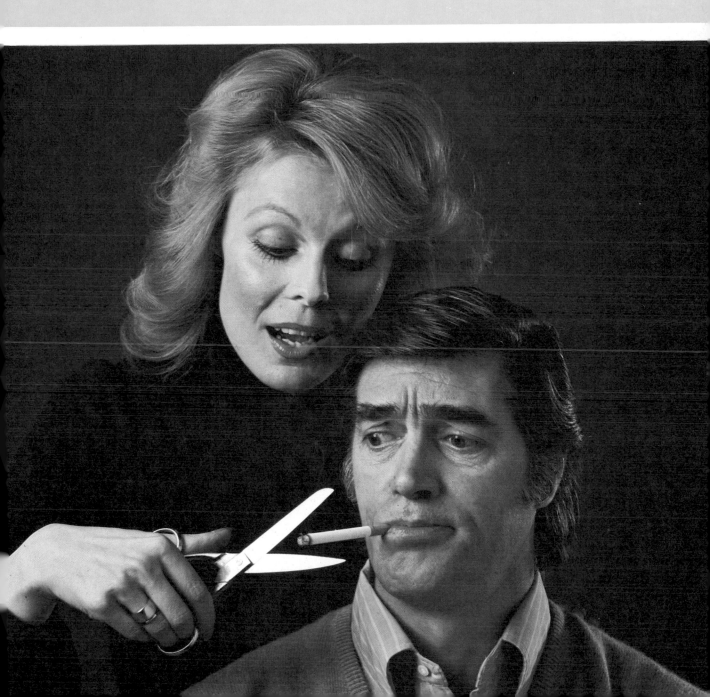

can't take the place of a father who is always working or who is too tired and harassed to play with his children or talk to his wife. It takes courage for a husband and wife to step back and reassess their life in these terms, but such a reassessment can sometimes be the key to happiness.

Of course, it isn't always possible—or even necessary—for a man to make such a major change in his way of life. Lots of men enjoy their work, and even for those who don't, changing jobs just for the sake of it isn't going to help. But there are other ways of relieving some of the inevitable tensions of everyday living. Take commuting, for example. Can your husband dodge the rush-hour crush by leaving home earlier in the morning? If this isn't practical, how about getting up sooner than you need anyway, so that the family can have an unrushed breakfast as a more relaxing start to the day. You will find it helps if you can manage to set the table, plan the breakfast menu (make it a cold one sometimes for speed), and get school supplies together the night before. Would your husband want you to make a few sandwiches for his lunch occasionally, so that he can avoid the noon-hour rush? Would an earlier or later lunch hour help? It helps, too, if

Left: long hours of
overworking, with little
time for rest or relaxa-
tion, can soon take their
toll of a man's health,
particularly if his job
is a stressful one.

Right: pottering in the
garden can be an ideal
way of relaxing from the
tensions of the workaday
world, and getting some
healthful exercise, too.

69

you can send your husband off with a cheery or a loving word in the morning—who knows, you might get the kind of response that will brighten your own day.

Whatever a man's job, it is important for him to get away from it altogether sometimes. If possible, says doctors, it is best for the whole family to take two short vacations a year instead of one long one. And they are all in favor of parents getting away together without the children every once in a while, if they can. But even the weekends can be a real change from routine with a little planning. And it is worth remembering that children often enjoy sharing an activity that Dad enjoys—a fishing trip, an outing to a local airport to watch the planes, or a couple of hours' gardening or carpentry, for example—better than a carefully organized expedition to the zoo or a museum which Dad may hate.

A variety of interests and activities can be the very best antidote to stress. And probably your husband will relax best by doing something completely removed from the preoccupations of everyday life. An absorbing spare-time activity can switch a man's mind away from his worries and may also give him an outlet for hidden talents and creative abilities that he cannot express in his work. Collecting coins, community politics, singing, painting, listening to music, playing cards, building model ships, puttering in the garden, or raising tropical fish: however serious or silly his hobby seems, it could be making all the difference to his life and health. If, on the other hand, your husband seems perfectly content without any obvious hobbies, all well and good. Watching TV, going to a ball-game once in a while, or an occasional evening out perhaps at a movie or theater may be all the relaxation he needs.

Relaxation, the key to well-being during the day, is also the key to a good night's sleep. That is why some of the time-honored ways of beating sleeplessness are often the best. Plenty of fresh air and exercise during the day, a soothing warm bath, a hot drink, and some music or light reading at bedtime are better than sleeping tablets. But if a man always has trouble getting to sleep—or staying asleep—he should, of course, seek the advice of a doctor. Doctoring himself with sleeping tablets can be dangerous.

Above all, it is important for a man not to worry about the sleep he is losing. Lying awake nights while the rest of the world slumbers is miserable, but it won't injure a man's health half as much as anxiety about not sleeping. In fact, say doctors, we could probably all do with a lot less sleep than we think we need. Long hours of sleep are for babies and teenagers, and too much sleep may be positively harmful to adult health. Sleep needs do, of course, vary from one person to another, but doctors generally advise that $7\frac{1}{2}$ hours sleep a night is quite sufficient for most men.

"Moderation in all things," then, seems to be the rule when it comes to guarding your husband's health. And very dull it may sound. But it may help to remind your husband of something Dr. Kinsey once wrote about a man's health. "Good health, sufficient exercise and sleep," he said, "still remain one of the most effective aphrodisiacs known to man." And remember, sex is also one of the best ways of relieving tension left to us in our present stress-filled world—as well as being one of the pleasures in life that won't do a thing to harm a man's health.

Caring for the Elderly
5

Taking a toddler out for walks is one activity that most grandparents are certain to enjoy. The pride and pleasure that elderly people take in their grandchildren is one of the factors that can contribute most to their continued zest for living. And they can often give much-needed time and attention to youngsters when busy parents need a break.

Annie is a spry 78-year-old. Elsie, the same age, is a frail old lady in failing health. Old age cannot be judged by years alone, and each person ages at a different rate. Yet, sooner or later, most of us will face the realization that someone close to us is getting old and may soon become dependent on our care and support. The wheel turns full circle until it is our turn to care for those who once looked after us. Along with our distress at seeing someone dearly loved becoming handicapped by age, we face inevitable and difficult questions: what should

we do about Grandma or Grandpa? How can we care for them best? Can they go on living alone? Should they come to live with us? What is the happiest solution for them and for all the family? And how can we make it work?

Joan was in no doubt over what she considered the right thing to do when an eye operation made it impossible for her elderly mother to live alone. Mama would come to live with her and husband Bill—and that was all there was to it. But it wasn't all. Joan's mother had disapproved of her marriage to

Greece 400 B.C.	30
Rome A.D. 600	30
Anglo-Saxon 800	31
England 1250	35
England 1450	33
England 1550	30
Massachusetts 1750	36
America 1850	38
America 1900	46
America 1940	60
America 1970	66

Left: people today live far longer and healthier lives than ever in the past. This diagram shows how much the average length of life has increased from long ago to recently. Below: "Those whom the gods love, die young," said the ancient Greeks and no wonder! The average life-span in those days was 30. Today, a man can look forward to at least 66 years, and may even live longer.

Bill, and, although she and her son-in-law managed to get along well enough during short visits, things were not so easy when they started living under the same roof. Deep down, Bill still resented his mother-in-law's former disapproval, and he couldn't always hide it.

"Try as I would," said Joan, "I couldn't seem to prevent the most innocent conversation from turning into a feud. I seemed to spend most of my time defending Bill to my mother, and my mother to Bill, and then I'd be irritable with them both. What made matters worse was that Mama had insisted on contributing most of her savings toward helping us buy our house. I think she felt it would make her more independent, but it made us feel that our home somehow wasn't altogether our own."

"Things finally came to a head over our little girl, Sandra, who is 11. Sandra hadn't done her homework one day, and Bill refused to let her go to a show with a friend's family. I think Bill meant to relent, but, in the meantime, he discovered that Mama had given Sandra some money and told her to go off and enjoy herself. I've never seen Bill so mad in my life. He shouted at my mother, and at me, and then slammed out of the house, saying if he couldn't be master in his own home, he'd be better off out of it."

This crisis forced Joan to a painful decision. "I decided I would have to tell my mother that I felt she wasn't as happy as I'd hoped living with us," said Joan, "and that perhaps we ought to consider some other solution. Mama reacted very badly at first, and refused to discuss the matter. But in the end it was her own suggestion that she move into a home for the elderly a few miles away. We can visit her two or three times a week, but she refuses point blank to see Bill when he comes. I feel terrible about the whole thing. Somehow we managed everything so completely wrong."

Commenting on a situation like this, Dr. William Poe, author of *The Old Person in Your Home,* says, "When an older relative is brought into a home where tensions already exist, the effects may be disastrous, sometimes without anyone's realizing just what is happening. This unhappy development can come about because the balance of power is upset—a concept as valid in the domestic area as in the family of nations." Threats to this balance may occur not only when a husband or wife does not get along with the elderly relative, but if, say, a wife and her mother seem so close that the husband feels left out, or if there are conflicts over decision-making, finance, disciplining the children, or other responsibilities in the home. "Conflicts should be recognized and if possible resolved before inviting an older person to move in," says Dr. Poe, ". . . If mother, father, and children can talk freely, if disagreement can occur without bitterness and obedience without resentment—then and only then should the older folks be invited into the household."

In such circumstances, having an elderly relative to live can be the best solution for all concerned. When the move is carefully thought out and planned for, it can work remarkably well. "Of course, adjustments have to be made," says Marjorie, whose mother-in-law has been living with her for five years, "not just at first, but all the time." Marjorie, her husband Dick, and their three children discussed the idea thoroughly before they asked Grandma to stay. "My main worry," remembers Marjorie, "was the fact that my two sons would have to share a bedroom. I was afraid they would resent this. But they agreed that, if Dick fixed up a screen in their room, they wouldn't mind too much. The children were very good with Grandma really, apart from the sort of minor squabbles you might expect, over their hair and clothes and that sort of thing. If it ever looked as though Grandma were going to interfere over the children, Dick would tell her jokingly that he took his role as head of the household very seriously and that he'd never manage it if he couldn't keep the kids in order his way.

"Naturally, I get annoyed when Grandma points out that there's a button missing on Dick's shirt, or that she always cooked her meals such-and-such a way. But I find it's best to patch up any disagreements as quickly as possible, even if it means backing down sometimes. After all, it can't be easy for her, living with us after having her own home, and I know she's desperately anxious not to interfere if she can help it. Call it luck, if you like, but I wouldn't have had things any other way. I think it's done our family good having Grandma here. And I'm sure my children have grown up more considerate because of it."

Of course, matters may be very different when an elderly relative needs a lot of nursing. Betty's 80-year-old father became housebound after a serious operation. He was just about able to manage in his own home at first, but he needed a lot of help. A visiting nurse called regularly, and a local voluntary organization sent a home visitor once a week. Betty paid for someone to clean her father's apartment and to cook him occasional light meals. She herself visited him each weekend, did his laundry, and provided food to reheat during the week.

After a while, however, her father's health deteriorated, and Betty found the considerable drain on her finances and her energy was becoming too great. She decided that the only solution was to have her father to live with her, even though this would mean giving up her part-time job in order to care for him. Betty took a short course in home nursing at her local Red Cross association, and was able to borrow some nursing equipment from another voluntary organization. "Another thing that helped," she says, "was finding that Dad was eligible for some home-health services under Medicare."

Thanks to a certain amount of outside help, Betty coped quite well for some time. "But nursing my father was a strain," she admits, "And I was desperately in need of a holiday. There was some question of Dad going into a hospital for a week while I took a break, but then he was taken seriously ill again and had to be transferred to hospital anyway. After that, my doctor said he thought it would be too much for me to look after Dad myself, and he suggested a nursing home, which is where my father is now."

Sometimes our elderly relatives don't need as much help as we think, and we may be overly concerned for their welfare in our anxiety to "do the right thing." Rita became very concerned about her 84-year-old widowed father after he had undergone an operation for prostate trouble. "I didn't think he should go on living alone, 800 miles away from us," she says, "But he was determined to stay in his own

Above left: alone and lonely, an elderly person who has no one left to care for, and no one to care for her, may live out a sad and aimless existence. Without some meaningful involvement in day-to-day activities and regular contact with others, she may lose all interest in life.

Above: a couple who grow old together have many shared memories to look back on, and can comfort and support each other during their later years. Right: continuing contact with children and grandchildren can help an elderly person feel that she still has a useful part to play in the life of the family.

familiar surroundings with people he knew. He said he could manage perfectly well with someone to clean for him a couple of times a week, and he has lots of friendly neighbors. But I was afraid that something might happen to him and then I would feel responsible." In fact, to Rita's surprise, after two years on his own, her father married a sprightly 80-year-old, and the two are still living in his home, ten years later.

Most doctors agree that it is far better for an elderly person to remain in his own home and in a familiar environment. Of the 22 million people in the United States over 65, two-thirds do live in their own homes, and a quarter of the others live with relatives. But what happens when neither solution is possible?

A reasonably active old person who does not feel confident about living alone, or who is forced to give up his home for financial reasons, may be able to rent a room in a private dwelling where meals are provided, so that he doesn't have to move from his own locality. This could also be the answer for an alert and independent-minded 75-year-old who won't hear of living "in one of those homes with a lot of old people." Special housing projects for senior citizens are another, fairly recent development that offers the independence of private living quarters along with the provision of meals, self-service laundries, shops, social activities, and medical facilities. The kind of services provided vary from project to project, and so does the cost. Centers operated by non-profit, tax-exempt organizations offer the most economical facilities, usually on a straight-lease basis. Then, of course, there are homes for the aged run by church denominations or fraternal organizations, and nursing homes that may be more suitable for old people who are less able to look after themselves, or who require nursing care.

Supposing you decide upon a nursing home, how can you tell if it is a good one? Unfortunately, the term "nursing home" can be confusing, as it may be used to cover many different types of facility that offer services ranging from strictly personal care and skilled nursing to hotel-like accommodation. To choose the kind of home that is best suited to your elderly relative's needs, therefore, it is wise to consult your doctor, or your local health and

welfare, or community service agency.

Find out if the home you are considering is officially licensed, about the services it offers, and the qualifications of the staff. Visit the home, unannounced if possible, and take a look at its facilities for yourself. Is the home cheerful, clean, and well-equipped? Does the staff seem kind and concerned? Is there enough staff? Are there adequate arrangements for medical and emergency care? What is the food like? Can the staff cope with special diets? Are plenty of activities organized for the residents? Chat with the patients, too. Do they seem reasonably contented and alert? What are the arrangements for visiting? Maybe you could talk to the families of other residents and get their impressions of the home. More questions like these can be found in the American Medical Association's Committee on Aging booklet called "What to Look for in a Nursing Home." And another source of information is the American Nursing Home Association.

One of the important questions you will be asking about a nursing home, of course, is the cost. How much? What does the price include? Is the home approved for Medicare benefits? In any discussion of where your elderly relative is to live, financial considerations are bound to play a big part. That is another reason why this needs to be a family discussion. Whatever arrangements are made for an aging parent, any financial burden should not have to rest on one member of the family alone. Can each adult in the family contribute so much a month according to his means? Find out all you can, too, about any financial aid to which Grandpa may be entitled. Check with your local welfare or Social Security office for information on medical, nursing home, and home-health benefits under Medicare and other government programs. Does Grandpa belong to any religious, fraternal, or union organizations that may be able to help?

Any family undertaking the care of an elderly person is likely to need outside help at some time. When considering where your elderly relative should live, don't forget to take into account services for the elderly that may be available in your (or his) community. Are

Right: aging starts sooner than we think. No one would deny that this man is getting on in years, but how about the children and young adults in the other pictures? Although still young and vigorous, they are already showing signs of aging— a continual process that begins at conception and goes on all through life. Different people age at different rates, of course, but the same overall process affects us all. But take heart! The over-30's can score over the youngsters when it comes to achievement. A famous study on age and creativity turned up these facts. The peak age for writing great poems is 30; for great novels, 45; for attaining an income of over $100,000, age 55; for becoming speaker of the House of Representatives, 75; for becoming Pope, 85 to 90.

there any voluntary organizations, or local chapters of such associations as the American Cancer Society, the American Heart Association, or the Arthritis Foundation, that could help with transportation to clinics, lend nursing equipment, or supply information on home care? Can you arrange for a visiting nurse to call, or is there a homemaker service that could supply nursing help at times of illness or stress? Check on the clubs and associations for the elderly in your area. Are there any day centers or senior workshops that could provide outside companionship and activities or work programs for use at home? Most states have official units on aging. Look up the nearest Information and Referral Service in your telephone directory, contact your local health and welfare council, or write for information and advice to the President's Council on Aging. One solution to avoid, however, is for members of the family to take turns in having Grandma live with them. This may be easier on individual members of the family, but poor Grandma will feel she has no real home anywhere.

When the care of an elderly person is in your hands, either because he lives alone or with you, you will be concerned to do all you can to ensure his health and happiness. And that means understanding something about the particular needs of the elderly.

Every old person is, of course, unique, but elderly people do share certain problems and anxieties. Apart from any physical discomfort they may be suffering, they worry about becoming a burden, about losing their ability to care

Before birth : A baby starts to age from the moment of conception. And it is interesting to note that, because a woman is born with a full complement of ova already in her ovaries, the egg from which her baby grows will probably be about 20, and possibly even 40, years old by the time it is fertilized.

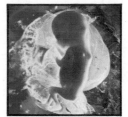

At birth : As the baby begins a separate life of his own, the first detectable signs of aging can be found. Wound-healing, for example, which is most effective at birth, becomes minutely less efficient from then on.

Age 7 : The blood vessels begin to show age changes, with the appearance of fatty deposits in the walls of the *aorta* (the main artery that carries the blood pumped out from the heart).

Age 8 : The eyes gradually begin to lose their ability to adjust automatically, and equally well, to vision at different distances. At this age, too, acuteness in hearing high notes begins to fall off very slightly.

Age 12 : This age marks a peak of health and vigor. Up to now, new tissues have kept ahead of the breakdown of old ones, thus enabling the body as a whole to increase in strength. If we could only stay as vigorous as we are at age 12, we should probably all live to the ripe old age of 700.

Age 25 : The first really important age changes, such as those that are just beginning to affect the walls of the arteries, may already be easy to detect. That is why doctors recommend that we should start having our regular medical checkups from this age on.

Age 30 : About now, muscle strength begins to decline, which is one reason why athletes may retire so young. However, endurance can compensate for strength. In fact, continuing exercise may in itself keep an older person's muscles working more efficiently than those of a less energetic 20-year-old.

Left: Grandma is still sure of an admiring audience when she gets out her box of treasures. Young children like to hear of Grandma's past —and Grandma will delight in telling it.

Right: Granny and grandchild have a happy knack of seeing eye-to-eye on most things. Older people will readily join in the make-believe and repetitive play that toddlers love, and are rewarded by the rapt attention they receive in return.

for themselves, about being useless or unwanted. They may be concerned about growing absent-mindedness, about being unable to cope with official papers, about lacking the money to meet their needs. They may find it difficult to make decisions, and be distressed by change. By being aware of such fears, we will find it easier to be patient and sympathetic. For old people need our love, and our reassurance of how much they are needed—and they are entitled to be treated with dignity and respect.

You will help Grandma feel needed if you encourage her to make full use of any special gifts she has, and if you show her how useful these are to you or others. Can she knit pullovers for the children, make clothes, or bake cakes—old-fashioned recipes are bound to be popular with the family. Maybe she could teach the children to sew dolls' dresses, knit cuddly toys, or make a batch of cookies. Could Grandpa help out in the garden, lend a hand with carpentry, show the children how to build

a model house, or take them out fishing?

If there is one thing old people are particularly good at, it is caring for small children. They are perfectly willing to tell the same story over and over again, to play repetitive games or take time to help a toddler dress or eat. And, for their part, children are the best confidence-boosters an elderly person could have. They will listen to Grandpa's stories without being patronising, happily pour out their own thoughts, and admire an old person's smallest talent. Similarly, it is a good idea if Grandpa can have a pet to care for, especially if he lives alone. A dog, a cat, or a bird will not only be a source of companionship and uncomplicated affection, but, above all, will be something that is dependent on him.

An elderly person will usually appreciate having some routine household job that is his province alone—doing the dishes or drying up, setting the table, peeling vegetables, sorting the laundry, mending, dusting, or tending the

80

window-box. Maybe Grandma will take twice as long over the task as you would, but do your best to curb the impulse to take over. The more an elderly person is encouraged to do, for himself and others, the better he will maintain his self-esteem and his good health. However, it is important not to ask him to do more than he can. This will mean a watchful eye on your part, but you will probably soon be able to judge if some task is getting out of hand, and find a tactful way of cutting down on some, though not all, of his duties.

Occasional mistakes and mishaps are bound to occur, but it doesn't help to criticize. Old people are only too aware of their short-comings. Criticism may make them lose more self-respect, and could even lead them to withdraw from all activity. Experts say that, when an accident occurs, it will help if you can take the blame yourself. In fact, old people may themselves look for scapegoats—their failing health, say, or even another member of the family—to take the blame when things go wrong, because they don't want to admit a loss of confidence in themselves. It would be a good idea to explain this to your children, in case Grandma seems to pick on them unfairly once in a while.

Old people tend to get muddled and forgetful, but their feelings are easily hurt. So it's wise to replace the need for too much decision-making with positive suggestions of your own. That doesn't mean that you should treat Grandma like a child. There is nothing most elderly people hate more (put yourself in their place!). Unless an old person is really ill, he doesn't want people fussing over him to help him eat or dress, no matter how slow or awkward he may be. But even if an elderly relative is dependent on you for his physical needs, he can still be made to feel respected and loved.

Grandpa has a right to be included in family conversations and to have his views heard along with everyone else's. He should know about Michael being at the top of his English class or Jill going away to summer camp, although you will, of course, want to spare him any worrying items of family news.

You may be disconcerted to find that one topic of great interest to Grandpa is death. Fear of death is usually strongest in the 55 to 65 age group. After 65, most people have come to terms with the idea of dying. But they do think about it a lot, and may be particularly anxious about where and how they are going to die. An elderly person may sometimes wish, and need, to discuss his death, arrangements for his funeral, and related topics that make the rest of the family feel uneasy and embarrassed. It doesn't help to say "Don't be silly, Mom, you're not going to die," or "Nonsense, Dad, you won't have to worry about that for a long time yet." Mom *is* going to die. Dad *is* worried. They're the ones who are being realistic, and they deserve our honest efforts to help. Far better, then, not to brush their concerns aside. If we are prepared to discuss death openly, we may be able to give them any positive reassurance they need.

Encourage members of the family to spend a little while chatting with Grandma as often as they can, and spare a few minutes for a chat when you provide a cup of coffee or a snack. It's a good idea, too, to provide a comfortable seat near a window that looks out onto the street, so that she can see what is going on outside. Help your elderly relative to keep up friendships, even if this means extra effort to get out and visit people or entertain them at home. Visits from a clergyman can also be very comforting to many elderly people.

Some old people prefer their own company, but mostly, like people of any age, they need the companionship of others. Sadly, their old friends may die or move away, leaving them lonely and isolated. That is why it is wise to encourage your elderly relative to belong to a club—not necessarily one designed for old folk, but maybe a special-interest club, where he can play chess or poker, discuss gardening or local history, with members of various ages. Golden age clubs or day centers for the elderly can also be excellent for providing the com-

For an elderly person living alone, the loyalty and devotion of a pet can be a great comfort. As well as being a source of companionship and affection, a pet can give her the satisfaction of having something that depends entirely on her love and care.

panionship of contemporaries, as well as shared activities. Some senior workshops may even provide paid work for the elderly that can be a great incentive for an old person as well as supplementing a slender income.

You can provide incentives for your elderly relative at home, too, for it is not enough to keep an elderly person busy if he always gets monotonous or pointless tasks to do. There's a lot of difference, for example, between knitting to pass the time and knitting some gloves specially for Johnny's birthday. Like the rest of us, elderly people will react with greater interest and enthusiasm if they are asked to make something *for* someone or for some special event. Birthdays, anniversaries, and other family celebrations can all provide exciting landmarks in an old person's year, and be goals that can be worked up to with plans and preparations.

An old person will probably also have his hobbies—reading, painting, writing letters, radio, TV, doing jigsaws, gardening, watching the birds come down for crumbs, fishing, walking, visiting friends or his club. A book on hobbies for the housebound could give you some good ideas on entertaining an elderly person who is at a loss to fill his time. Remember, however, that old people tire easily, so lots of short conversations and visits or TV programs are best. You can make his life easier, too, by providing strong lighting, bigger print books, and clear lettering on telephone dials, as well as making sure that this surroundings are safe (see pages 96, 98).

A short vacation, maybe with another relative, could work well, but this should be planned carefully. Elderly people generally find sudden changes distressing. They need plenty of warning of any change and what it involves, and they hate to be hurried. That is why regular weekly outings are usually happier for them than longer-term upheavals that disrupt a comforting routine. And when an elderly per-

son has to move from his familiar surroundings, it is important to make sure he can take something of his old world along—books, pictures, or furniture, for example.

Activities are important to ensure that an elderly person gets the exercise he needs. For, although aging reduces reserves of strength and energy, exercise is still necessary to keep muscles active and maintain good health. Moderation is, as usual, the keynote here. Sudden or prolonged exercise is out, and exercise should never be continued after any signs of tiredness. Walking is still probably the best exercise for the elderly, but old people who have been used to swimming, dancing, gardening, bicycling, playing golf or bowls, can safely continue this, in small doses.

Encourage a less active elderly person to get some exercise by helping as much as he can around the house—even making coffee or pottering in the garden are helpful if more strenuous exercise is impossible. An old person should never be confined to bed unless illness makes this absolutely necessary. In this case, or where an elderly person is housebound, the doctor or an association for the elderly may be able to suggest a few simple exercises to be done each day. And don't forget the therapeutic value of laughter, says Dr. Siegmund H. May. Laughing, it seems, is actually good for us physically as well as psychologically. A European anatomist has worked out that the simple act of laughing sets in motion no less than 26 muscles, as well as multiplying air exchange in the lungs seven times.

Plenty of activity during the day will also help an old person to sleep at night. Older people tend to sleep less and wake more often during the night than we do. But if your elderly relative has trouble sleeping, try providing little breaks in routine during the day. Avoid leaving Grandpa alone too much, or make sure that he has something to keep him occupied while he is alone, so that he won't be tempted to take too many daytime naps. His bed should, of course, be made as comfortable as possible, and it is important that the bathroom be near at hand. A warm, milky drink before bed is a help, but remember that sleeping tablets,

The later years can be both purposeful and rewarding, as many of the well-known have shown.

Above: Queen Victoria, the longest-reigning British monarch. Mother of nine, she ruled for 63 years, giving her name to an era that saw Great Britain at the height of its power.

Right: John Davison Rockefeller, once the world's richest man. He lived to the age of 98, devoting the latter years of his life to the foundations through which he donated well over $500 million from the fortune he had made in the oil industry and world trade.

Above: Bertrand Russell, British mathematician and philosopher. A lifelong pacifist, he was leading moves to ban nuclear weapons when he was in his nineties.

Below: Albert Schweitzer, German philosopher and medical missionary. He won a Nobel prize at age 77, and devoted the proceeds to keeping up his African hospital.

Above: Rose Kennedy, pictured here at the age of 78, is glowing proof that the art of aging beautifully lies in maintaining a vigoros mental outlook and continuing to lead a busy life, with physical exercise, too.

Left: Grandma Moses, who had never had an art lesson in her life, began a new career as a painter at the age of 76. Although suffering from arthritis, she remained active until her death 25 years later.

85

Danger Signals

Seeing flashes of light before the eyes
Seeing double
Failing sight
Seeing haloes surrounding objects
Pain in the eye

Hearing loss
Reduced effectiveness of a hearing aid

Spots or sores on the skin which
enlarge or bleed
Irritation or sudden dryness of the skin
A lump anywhere, particularly in the breast

Pain or discoloration of the toes or forefoot
Pins and needles or numbness of feet,
hands, or face
Weakness of the muscles of the face
Loss of power in an arm or leg
Persistent trembling or shaking
Pain, swelling, or stiffness in a joint or bone
Pain in the calf of the leg, particularly on
walking

Breathlessness
Pain in the chest, arm, or throat
Persistent cough or hoarseness
Coughing blood

Loss of appetite
Difficulty in swallowing
Dry mouth or excessive thirst
Unexplained loss of weight
Persistent indigestion
Vomiting blood

Altered bowel habit
Persistent constipation or diarrhea
Passing blood from the bowel
Blood in the urine
Difficulty in urinating
Increased frequency and urgency of
urination
Itching around the genitals
Vaginal bleeding

Falling or unsteadiness
Giddiness
Feeling lightheaded or faint

Unnatural tiredness
Altered sleep pattern

Marked deterioration of memory
Confusion, especially at night
Feeling of despondency, hopelessness
or persecution
Noticeable change of mental attitude

particularly barbiturates, can be dangerous for the elderly. Not only may they be habit-forming if taken regularly, but an elderly person can easily forget how many tablets he has taken, or get up during the night in a muddled state because of the tablets, and suffer a fall. Sleeping drugs should therefore never be taken except when prescribed by a doctor, and should not be left on a bedside table.

The elderly need less food than more active younger people, but they must eat the right things (see page 28). A poor diet, especially one lacking in vitamins, can cause all sorts of health problems, from difficulty in swallowing and digestive upsets to loss of appetite and fatigue. Elderly people need plenty of protein (principally from meat, fish, cheese, eggs and milk) to replace worn-out tissues, and lots of vitamins from fruit and vegetables. (A casserole containing meat and vegetables is ideal fare for a person living alone as it is nutritious and easily reheated.) Older people should cut down on fats, which may slow their less efficient digestion, and on carbohydrates (an old person needs less of the energy that these provide, and starchy or sugary foods may spoil his appetite for more essential foods). Their diet should be rich in calcium (mainly from milk and cheese) and contain Vitamin D sources like fish-liver oils and margarine to counteract softened or brittle bones. They also need plenty of fluids—around two quarts a day—to aid digestion and help clear waste products from the kidneys. As appetite may lessen with age and sense of taste and smell become less sharp, food should be as varied as possible, look attractive, and be well seasoned. Even elderly people who have difficulty chewing food need not have an endless succession of ground meat—finely-sliced meat, fish, egg dishes, soft cheese, risottos, or stuffed vegetables could be welcome variations. And a glass of wine or jigger of alcohol before dinner can help stimulate a flagging appetite.

Even a vigorous and healthy old person

An elderly relative may be slow to report signs of ill health, and others must keep an eye out for his welfare. Here are some of the symptoms that may occur and always need speedy medical attention.

should continue to have a medical checkup once a year. Making an appointment on their birthday helps some people to remember. Regular dental care is also important, and so are checks on vision and hearing. Even if a person wears dentures, these will need to be adjusted or replaced as the shape of his mouth alters. A home dental service is available through some district and county societies of the American Dental Association. If your elderly relative requires a hearing aid, make sure he is referred to a nonprofit hearing clinic by his doctor, rather than buying an aid directly from a dealer.

Old people are often reluctant to report symptoms of illness, either from shyness, hopelessness, fear of going to the hospital, of upsetting relatives or being a nuisance, or maybe because their doctor has seemed unsympathetic in the past. So it is important for us to be on the alert for any signs of illness in our elderly relatives (see page 86). Don't be too willing to put symptoms, such as dizziness, breathlessness, aches and pains, indigestion, or fatigue, down to "old age"—they may indicate some illness that can be diagnosed and cured.

It is not easy to be old in our society. In a culture that is youth-oriented and that places a high value on productivity, the old may feel alienated, underprivileged, unwanted. The old need food, clothing, shelter, medical care. But, like all of us, they also need to be involved in meaningful daily activities, and, above all, they need someone to love. Questioned recently about the factors that contribute most to contentment in their later years, a group of elderly people were unanimous in placing family contacts and solidarity top of the list. And doctors who work with the elderly know that the mutual support of family members is a major factor in prolonging physical and mental independence in older people. Here, then, is how we can care for the elderly best—by showing them the loving concern that will bring joy and comfort to their lives.

Between these two, the generation gap is surely bridged. Grandpa can feel himself in harmony with his little girl, and she in turn will benefit from the sense of continuity he brings to her everyday life.

Safety in the Home

6

The house has been unusually quiet for the last ten minutes. The children seem to be playing peacefully for a change. You are busy in the kitchen. Suddenly, there is a thud from the next room and a piercing shriek from one of your children. Your heart goes cold. As you rush in, your thoughts race too. What has happened? How bad is it? What will you have to do?

What a relief, then, to find that it is nothing more than a banged head or a bumped knee. Your child is frightened. He needs a lot of cuddling and soothing. But he isn't badly hurt.

Most of the time, that's the way it is. Bathing cuts and grazes, drying up tears, and soothing the pain away are part of every mother's life. But, sadly, it isn't always like that. Each year, in the United States alone, around 18 million children—or one child out of every three—are seriously hurt or killed in accidents, more than half of which occur at home.

Horrifying, isn't it? Yet every one of these tragic accidents could almost certainly have been avoided. Most of us just go on hoping such tragedies won't happen to us. But every time we put off some tiresome or seemingly expensive precaution, we could be placing our family at risk from a serious or even fatal accident that need not happen.

That's not to say that you should sit there fretting over every accident that could possibly befall your family. Of course, if you give Johnny a pair of roller skates, he might lose control of them, and he might run into a wall, and he could lose his front teeth or knock himself out. But Johnny also has to enjoy himself, and only by collecting a few bumps and bruises can a child learn to protect himself from more serious accidents later. Over-protecting a child prevents him from having this chance to learn,

and may even make him so fearful that he actually becomes "accident-prone." Somehow we have to strike a balance between over-protectiveness and reasonable care. So how's it done? How can you help your family to avoid accidents without being a fuss-budget? And do you know how to cope if an accident does happen?

Above all, it is important to be aware of the dangers that may lurk in and around your home

Right: to a toddler, a saucepan handle sticking out just above her head is simply asking to be pulled down and inspected, usually with disastrous results.

Below: brightly-colored pills and sugar-coated tablets may look just like candies to a curious child.

(see page 97). Such dangers are a threat to all the family, but each member, according to his age, capacities, or activity in the home, may be more at risk from some hazards than from others.

Take baby, for example. He is usually the best protected member of the family. But, sadly, accidents do happen to babies. The greatest hazard they face is choking, and this may happen when a busy mother leaves her baby alone to feed with a propped-up bottle. The baby has no way of stopping the flow of milk and may all too easily choke. A baby can also choke if he brings back a feed in his crib and inhales it because he just isn't able to turn away. You can keep your baby safe from this risk by leaving him on his side or stomach—not on his back. Remember, too, that babies under a year don't need a pillow.

Scalds are another hazard for babies. It may be that the one time you forget to test your baby's milk or his bathwater, it will turn out to be too hot. Or you could just be passing a cup of coffee to your husband, over the baby's head, when he decides to give Dad a friendly wave. For baby's bath, the elbow test is still the best. Hands are too tough and might not tell you when the water is too hot. Put the cold water in before the hot, and keep baby away from taps he could accidentally strike and turn on. And, of course, never leave your baby alone in the bath for a second. If you have forgotten the towel, you will just have to take a dripping baby along on the search.

Another place not to leave your baby alone is on a table, an adult bed, or any other high place where he is unprotected. He can be off that perch in a flash. And while a fall might not harm him too much, there is no point in your

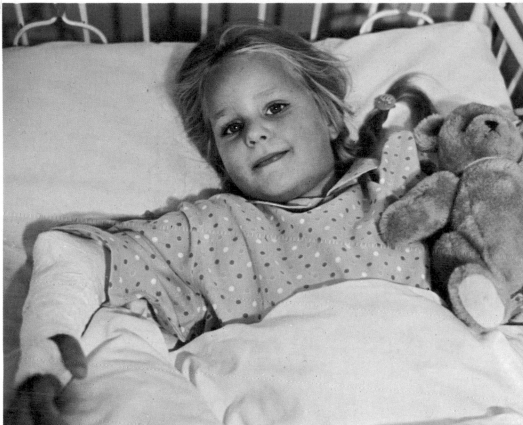

Left: a family outing doesn't always work out as planned. While Dad's back is turned, the children can find more dangerous ways to enjoy themselves. Below: the sad end to one child's adventurous day. Parents can't always be there to prevent accidents, so it helps if they teach their children safety.

being a candidate for the treatment of shock. Be wise, too, about buying a carriage, playpen, crib, or high-chair that carries a safety label, and test such equipment thoroughly for stability before you buy.

The baby who was generally content to kick his legs in the air and coo all too soon becomes an avid explorer who is fully mobile and into everything. Blissfully unaware of danger, he wants to touch, squeeze, throw, listen to, test out, lick, or taste anything he can find. The years from one to three have been called the "age of accidents," and here's where your real problems begin, safety-wise. For while you can't, and mustn't, keep this eager little adventurer confined, you have to keep the world he is exploring as safe as possible.

By far the commonest threat to toddlers is poisoning. More than half a million pre-schoolers are poisoned in their own homes every year. The average home is filled with poisons. Not sinister little phials of arsenic or cyanide, but ordinary detergents, disinfectants, oven cleaners, paint, kerosene, spot removers, and all kinds of household cleansers. Even hair spray and makeup can be dangerous in the hands of a child. Banish these poisons to high-up shelves, or lock them up.

Brightly-colored drugs and medicines, too, are almost bound to catch a toddler's eye. Three-year-old Timothy, for example, helped himself to a handful of candies while his mother's back was turned. Only the candies weren't candies—they were sleeping tablets. Jane, $2\frac{1}{2}$, had seen her mother taking some medicine and wanted to copy. She had swallowed half a bottle of laxative before her mother arrived on the scene. The only safe way is to

91

Happy and secure in mother's arms, this baby is safe enough from danger. But he will also need her care and foresight later on to protect him when she is not around and he inevitably starts exploring for himself.

keep all drugs and medicines securely under lock and key, and out of sight of any child under 8 or 9. As your child gets older, you can begin to teach him about the safe use of home remedies and cleaning materials.

Comes the day when Dad finally gets around to repainting little Johnny's bedroom. But before you raise a cheer, remember to check that the paint he is going to use carries a label saying that that it is safe for use on surfaces that might be licked or chewed by children. Look for the safety label, too, on toys and furniture, and make sure that your child's toys have no detachable parts he could pop in his mouth.

Imagine yourself at child level and check household fixtures for safety even before your baby starts to crawl or takes his first steps. Are low tables free of ashtrays or other heavy objects that he could pull down on his head? Are any electric cords dangling within his reach? Could he get at the electric sockets? He probably would not be able to stick his fingers far enough into the sockets for danger, but he might push some metal object into the holes,

A baby left unprotected on a bed, chair, or any high place could scramble or topple off in a flash.

Check your baby's playpen for safety before you buy. Bars that are too close could jam his head.

Always test baby's bath water—the elbow test is best—and put the cold water in before the hot.

with disastrous results. Either block access to sockets with a heavy piece of furniture, or better still, fit them with childproof safety plugs.

Be careful to keep all plastic coverings in a child-proof place—a child can suffocate in seconds if he puts a plastic bag over his head. And while it might seem like a good idea to use the plastic coverings from the dry-cleaners to protect the mattress of a child's bed, don't try it. Even a fragment of polythene could catch in a child's throat and choke him. All small items like pins, screws, nails, earrings, or cuff-links, should also be well out of your child's reach.

Remove whatever dangerous objects you can from your child's path, and be on the alert to protect him from those that have to remain. Remember, warning a toddler isn't enough. At this age, you need to remove him firmly and consistently from danger. If he still wanders back, try giving him something safer to play with. If he seems bent on playing with forbidden items, check that he is having sufficient freedom and attention from you in other ways.

The kitchen, with its gadgets and appliances, is a number-one danger zone for inquisitive toddlers, and some accident prevention experts recommend keeping small children out of the kitchen altogether. However, it is almost certainly more practical for most mothers to set up a safe play area in the kitchen. You don't need a lot of space. Even a low drawer containing wooden spoons, plastic bowls, and other safe items of kitchen equipment, or a cardboard carton stocked with some of his toys should be enough to amuse your toddler while you work.

The kitchen should, however, be out of bounds to your toddler when you are cleaning with buckets of hot water or transferring hot food from stove to plates. And do check that appliances are switched off before you leave the kitchen and saucepan handles always turned away from the edge of the stove. Knives, scissors, and other everyday tools are also best kept out of reach, but around the age of two or three, you could begin to teach your child to cope with the dangers of these by showing him how to use them in safe, simplified versions. The same goes for matches and cigarette lighters. Many bad fires start when children play with these, so it's best to keep them right away from temptation. Later you can teach your child how to use them safely—maybe by letting him help to light candles or a bonfire, under your strict supervision. Remember, too, that non- or low-flammable fabrics are a wise buy when you have tots around the house.

Play safe with plastic bags and coverings. A child could suffocate if he puts one over his head.

A garbage pail is a triple hazard: its contents can cut or poison as well as spreading germs.

Electric cords should be out of reach. One small tug could bring the iron down on baby's head.

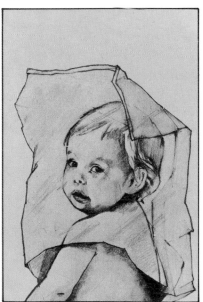
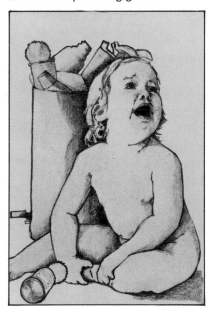
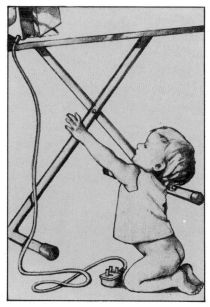

Falls are still a hazard for the toddler who is none too steady on his feet. Most of these are minor tumbles, and even quite a hard wallop may cause little harm because children's bones are so much more supple and resilient than ours. According to one doctor, the average toddler will have at least "one good fall" a month. But prevent your child from raising his average to danger level by fixing safety gates across the top of the stairs and safety catches to windows. Balconies, too, should be free of chairs or boxes that your child might scramble onto.

Safety begins at home. But active older toddlers will be out and about more than ever, and that means keeping an eye on the environment around your home, too. Has your child got a safe place where he can run about and climb? Is your yard securely fenced off and free of dangers such as planks with nails sticking out, rusty machinery, or garden tools? Does your garage have a childproof fastening, and have you removed the catch or door from a disused refrigerator put aside for storage?

Many are the children who have received nasty bites and stings by saying "hello" to unappreciative animals and insects. So teach your children early that strange cats or dogs are not so amenable to having their tails pulled as their own home pet might be. Use picture books or a family jaunt to teach them the distinctive markings of poisonous insects and berries.

The roving preschooler rarely fears water, and has little idea of its depth, so don't let your child out of sight for a moment at the beach, near a river or lake, or even at the swimming pool. If you have a garden pool, fit it with an electric pool alarm or with fencing and locked gates. Remember to empty wading pools out as soon as your children have finished playing. Even two inches of water could drown a child.

This is also the age to teach your children road safety. And your example is the best way to do it. Observe the rules of the road when you are out with your toddler—even if it means an annoying detour to cross in a safe place—and get him to repeat the rules as you go. Practice safe driving, too, and fit your car with children's safety seats or belts, and childproof locks. Children should be out of harm's way in the back seat of the car, and they will need toys to keep them busy. If they do get fidgety and misbehave, it's best to stop and get them settled before driving on. Of course, it is tempting fate to leave a parked car unlocked or to leave your children alone inside. Be sure, too, to find out where your child is before you back the car out of your garage or driveway.

It may seem tough work supervising the safety of your preschooler, but what happens when he gets to the age of streetplay, bike-riding, tree-climbing, and exploring "forbidden ground"? Is there anything you can do to keep him safe beyond biting your lip and hoping for the best? Yes, say accident prevention experts.

Above: electric cords, plugs, and sockets could be a trap for a toddler who doesn't yet know where danger lies. He may poke his fingers into unprotected sockets, or try to put in plugs as he has seen his parents do. The safe way is to keep cords out of reach, replace them when they fray, and fit sockets within his reach with special safety plugs.

Right: it isn't enough for drugs and medicines to be out of reach if an inquisitive young child can still get at them. The medicine chest should always be kept securely locked with a childproof fastening.

Say "no" to play in busy streets, and warn your child to stay away from nearby reservoirs, canals, quarries, dumps, demolition sites, or disused houses. Explain exactly why such places are dangerous. But, knowing that your youngster is likely to be fascinated by these areas just the same, try to ensure that he has plenty of other, safer ways to find adventure—in parks, playgrounds, and recreation areas, through family outings and club activities. Join with other parents to promote safety for children in your community.

If possible, even before your child gets on a bike, teach him traffic rules and road signals until he knows them by heart. Children's books can help you here, and you could make a game of asking your child to interpret traffic signals when he is out with you in the car. If there is a road safety or cycling proficiency course for children in your community, all the better.

Within the home, too, there are still some precautions to be taken. If you must have a gun in the house, for example, do remember to keep it unloaded and securely locked away—firearms are a major cause of accidental death in the 10 to 14 age group.

The best way of all to protect your growing child is to teach him how to cope with danger. Don't be content with lectures and warnings. Show him how to do things safely—to cross a

street, use a washing machine, handle a kitchen knife, climb a tree. Explain the dangers involved, but give him plenty of practice with you on hand to guide him. And always do things the safe way yourself—if you take risks, so will he.

Children are not, of course, the only ones at risk from accidents. Elderly people are particu-larly vulnerable to accidents in the home—accidents that we can help to prevent. Protect the elderly members of your family by fixing obvious hazards around the house—broken steps or furniture, wobbly handrails, fraying carpets, or trailing electric cords. Even minor falls can severely injure an old person whose bones are frailer than ours. Choose non-slip

Dangers in the Home

Millions of Americans, especially children, are killed or injured every year as a result of accidents in their own home. How safe is your house ? The simplest way to find out is to take an occasional walk around it—both you and your husband if possible—and look out for probable hazards like those shown below

1. Could your child get up into the attic ? Are ladders safe for adults ?
2. Are windows guarded or have safety locks ?
3. Are plastic bags well out of children's reach ?
4. Do you keep cosmetics out of their reach ?
5. Is your staircase fitted with safety gates ?
6. Have any toys or cleaning materials been left on the stairs where they could cause a fall ?
7. Are water splashes dried to avoid slipping ?
8. Is your garage locked to keep the children out ?
9. Are electric cords frayed ? Could your children get at them ? Do you use safety plugs ?
10. Are Dad's gun and ammunition locked up ?
11. If you ever have an open fire, do you make sure it is well guarded ?
12. Some house plants are poisonous if eaten by children. Are yours ?
13. Do you keep alcohol under lock and key ?
14. Could Dad doze off while smoking ? Is his lighter or matches out of reach of small children ?
15. Do you always turn pot handles away from the edge of the stove ?
16. Are kitchen tools out of toddlers' reach ?
17. Do you mop up spills at once, before a fall ?
18. Do you use non slip polishes on all floors ?
19. Is your garbage pail covered by a locking lid ?
20. Could your child get at washing machine or dryer when he's alone ?
21. Are detergents kept out of children's reach ?
22. Is your freezer fitted with a safety catch ?
23. How about the garden or yard ? If you have a pool, is it fenced in and locked ? Are fences safe ? Tools locked away ? Outdoor toys in safe shape ? Nothing dangerous left lying around ?

carpets and floor polishes, and mop up spills at once before they cause a fall. A vacuum cleaner, brushes, or toys left around on the stairs are another trap for the elderly. Try to encourage your child from an early age to put his toys away at the end of each day's play by getting him to help you stack them into his own special toy-box (any old crate or carton will serve the purpose). Strong lighting is another "must" for the elderly, and lights that can be operated both from the bottom and top of stairs are particularly useful. Prevent accidents in the bathroom by putting a rubber mat in the tub or shower, and installing hand-rails by the bath and toilet.

Poisoning is a big risk for elderly people, who may get muddled over the number of sleeping tablets they have taken, or misread directions on bottles or packets. Keep them safe by labeling drugs in big, easy-to-read letters, or putting out a single dose of medicine before going to bed and locking the rest away. Even an independent-minded Grandma is bound to understand that you are anxious to keep drugs safely away from children. Remember, too, to throw away all medicines, once treatment is over, by flushing them down the toilet. Left-over medicines may not only become less effective after a time, but can be positively harmful.

Asked which member of the family is *least* likely to have an accident in the house, most of us would probably say our husband. After all, he generally spends less time at home than anyone else. But, surprisingly, many more men than women are killed by accidents in their own homes. Why? The answer may lie in the sort of accidents they have—electrocution, falls, and burns. These happen mostly during do-it-yourself operations around the house. Don't we all tend to leave any dangerous or difficult home maintenance jobs to a man, be it fixing the iron, repairing the oil burner, painting the ceiling, or heaving an old piece of furniture down into the basement? All too often, men do these jobs in a hurry, or when they are already tired or irritated at the end of the day. And, of course, some men may tackle such jobs carelessly or without all the necessary know-how.

This doesn't mean that you have to take over

A pet can be a child's best friend, teaching him gentleness and a sense of responsibility, as well as providing companionship and fun. For safety's sake, pick a pet that comes from a reputable store, and avoid baby wild animals or full-grown pets that are not used to children. Teach your child the right way to handle and care for the family pet, but warn him that strange animals might not be as friendly as his own, and should not be approached.

home repairs in addition to all your other chores. There is no point in your falling off a ladder instead of your husband. But you can make sure the ladder is safe before either of you uses it. If it is rickety with age, it's worth buying a new one—now. The same goes for broken plugs or frayed cords. Don't hesitate to throw them out and buy new ones. It's easy, too, to check on the safety of stairs, steps, and railings while you are cleaning the house. Your husband may be able to fix any that are loose, but you can keep an eye out for what needs fixing before he trips over it. And when it comes to the fixing, most of us can soon learn enough to lend a hand with plumbing repairs, car maintenance, and replacing fuses. It's no fun hovering in the background holding the screwdriver, or popping in and out with a nervous "Do be careful, dear." Better by far to pick up information that might prove invaluable some day when we have to do our own repairs.

Expecting a man to be an automatic expert at household repairs is like thinking all women are born superb cooks. Some men just aren't good at repairs. But they may feel pressured into tackling an over-ambitious project for pride's sake. Sam's neighbor had rewired his house to save money, and Sam decided to do the same. He received a severe electric shock and died. Another man who had never set foot on a roof, tried to retile part of his house, and fell, breaking his arm and leg. So unless your husband has the know-how and experience to handle major installations or repairs, it is wise to call in a professional. Better a builder's invoice, after all, than a bill from the local hospital.

Above all, it is wise not to ask your husband to fix something when he is already tired. You have probably noticed how much more "accident-prone" you are when you are tired or cross, and even the most methodical and careful man is going to be less efficient by the time he gets home in the evening. So, unless that repair just can't wait until the weekend, play safe.

Maybe you are less likely to have a household accident than your husband, but just because you're an expert at steering your way around dangers in your home, it doesn't mean that you should take risks. Even if *you* want to tempt fate—perhaps by taking hazardous short-cuts—you may be putting other members of the family at risk. Your example plays a big part in teaching your family safety. And, most of all, they need you, remember?

There probably isn't one of us who hasn't sometimes climbed onto the nearest chair, instead of using household steps, to get at a high shelf or unhook a curtain—a common cause of bad falls. And all too often we keep heavy pans on the highest shelves so that lifting them down becomes doubly dangerous. Wearing our oldest clothes around the house seems like a good idea, but loose or worn shoes can easily make you trip, and torn seams, big pockets, or trailing apron strings may catch on a chair or door handle just when you are maneuvering a trayful of food into the room.

Have you ever washed the beaters of an

Emergency!

1. Keep calm.
2. Protect yourself before trying to help. (Touching an electric shock victim before switching off the current, for example, could make you a casualty, too.)
3. Don't move a badly injured person, unless he is threatened by further serious danger.
4. Check that the casualty is breathing. If not, immediately start mouth-to-mouth resuscitation.
5. Stop any serious bleeding by direct pressure on the wound. Check for severe injury before treating any obvious minor cuts.
6. If the person is breathing but unconscious, place him in the "coma position" (see page 141) to prevent choking.
7. Send for medical help—get someone else to do this if you can.
8. Give nothing whatever to eat or drink (except in certain cases of serious burns or poisoning, see pages 138, 139).
9. Treat for shock (see page 132).
10. Comfort and reassure the person. Don't leave him alone unless you absolutely must.
11. Most important of all, if you don't know what to do, *do nothing,* apart from getting medical help *fast.*

Above: whatever the emergency you face, following these simple rules will help you cope efficiently. Right: knowing these rules, and enough first aid to help carry them out, could prevent even a serious household accident from becoming a tragedy.

electric mixer under the tap without unplugging the mixer first? And do you remember to switch off the electric range before cleaning it? Electric currents and water are two things to keep strictly apart. So don't touch electrical appliances with wet hands, clean switches or sockets without turning off electricity at the main switch, or stand on a wet floor while you do the ironing. Keep yourself and your family safe, too, by buying well-designed household equipment made to approved standards of quality and safety. Follow the instructions to the letter, and have electrical appliances serviced regularly.

No matter how careful you are, however, the

Your Medicine Chest

First-aid supplies	Other medical supplies
Adhesive bandages – assorted sizes	Clinical thermometers – one oral, one rectal
Roll bandage – 2 inches wide	Electric vaporizer – cool mist type, for croup and breathing difficulties
Elastic bandage – 3 inches wide, for sprains	Hot-water bottle or electric heating pad
Sterile gauze pads – 4 inches square	Aspirin – regular 5-grain tablets
Adhesive tape	Children's aspirin – $1\frac{1}{4}$-grain tablets
Sterile absorbent cotton – $\frac{1}{2}$ oz. box	Calcium carbonate or a proprietary antacid containing calcium carbonate, aluminum hydroxide, and a magnesium salt – for indigestion
Scissors	
Safety pins	
Tweezers, with fine points, and needles – for splinters	A mild laxative – milk of magnesia, cascara sagrada extract tablets, or senna tablets, for occasional use
Syrup of Ipecac – ready-packed in doses, to induce vomiting in certain cases of poisoning	
Powdered activated charcoal, or "Universal Antidote" – against poisoning	Lozenges (blackcurrant, peppermint, etc.) – for sore throat or tickling cough
Antiseptic – isopropyl (rubbing) alcohol	Calamine lotion – for itching skin
Ice bag – for injured joints and muscles	Zinc ointment – for sore, moist skin
First-aid manual	Lanolin cream – for sore, dry skin
Phone number list – day and night no. of doctor, Poison Control Center, ambulance, pharmacist, fire department, police, etc.	

day may come when you find yourself faced with a really serious emergency. Your husband cuts himself badly with an electric saw. Grandfather has a stroke. Your child swallows nail polish remover. Their survival depends on you. Do you know what to do to save their lives?

The very idea of such a situation is likely to strike panic in the hearts of most of us. And that is why it is so important to learn what to do in advance. The best way to learn is by taking a Red Cross class or an adult education course in first-aid. If you cannot take a class, buy a first-aid handbook and study it *before* an accident happens. Knowledge like this will help to give you the confidence you need in a crisis —confidence that will comfort the patient, too.

Details of how to deal with particular emer-gencies appear at the end of this book, but whatever the emergency you face, following a few simple rules can help to see you through (see page 100). You should, of course, also have some basic first-aid supplies on hand. A list of the items you need appears above, together with suggestions for other supplies to meet less urgent medical problems that may crop up in your family. Save money when stocking your medicine chest by buying drugs under their generic, rather than their brand name. Both branded and non-branded drugs conform to the U.S.P. (United States Pharmacopoeia) or N.F. (National Formulary) standards for identity, purity, and strength, but the generic-name drug usually costs less.

Apart from medical supplies, your first-aid

Basic first-aid kit for the car

Roll bandage – 2 inches wide
Elastic bandage – 3 inches wide
Sterile gauze pads – 4 inches square
Cotton sheeting – 4 feet square, for a sling
Safety pins
First-aid manual

Left: a well-equipped medicine chest is a must for dealing with emergencies and treating the minor illnesses that may occur in any family. Here are details of the first-aid materials and basic medical supplies that you should have on hand at home and a short-list of items to keep in the car.

Below: with the right materials to hand, and a knowledge of first-aid, a mother can cope in a crisis and still be calm enough to give the soothing reassurance that is often the best medicine.

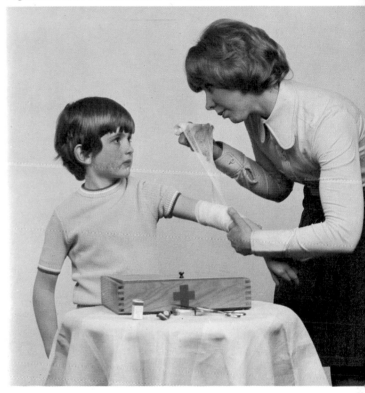

box should contain a first-aid manual (the Red Cross produces an excellent one), and the vital telephone numbers you may need in a crisis—the day and night number of your doctor, the nearest Poison Control Center, ambulance, pharmacist, fire department, police, and the number of a neighbor who could hold the fort in an emergency. Keep these numbers near the phone, too—maybe pinned to the wall or pasted to the telephone table—to save seconds that might be vital. Note down clearly who to call for what, and the number of anyone you think you might need in an emergency. Even jot down your husband's work telephone number—panic can make the best-known numbers fly out of your mind, and if you leave a neighbor in charge while you go to the hospital, she will know how to contact him. Don't forget to replace used first-aid supplies and to put scissors back after use.

A smaller set of essential first-aid supplies (abova left) should be kept in your car. And make sure your family carries information that will help if they meet with an accident away from home—blood group, if diabetic, if allergic to certain medicines, name, address, phone number, details of who to contact in case of accident, and so on.

With precautions like these to prevent and cope with accidents, you can rest assured that you have done your utmost to protect your family and to ensure that, whatever danger they encounter, they have the very best chance of coming through safe and sound.

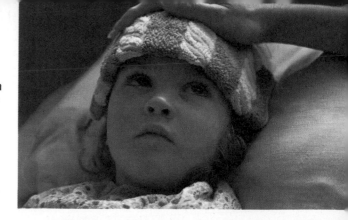

Right: a cool compress on his forehead can soothe a child who has a high fever, and may also be helpful in bringing down his temperature. Below: sometimes the symptoms of illness are not quite so obvious. A sick child may simply seem listless, lethargic, and not her usual self.

When the Children Get Sick

7

A mild rash or a case of measles? Appendicitis or too many ice creams? A slight sore throat or the start of an infection? Children can seem very ill with something mild, but they can also become seriously ill very quickly. As if that weren't enough, worrying symptoms have a habit of getting worse late at night, so that, on top of your anxiety about your child, you may worry about whether or not to call your doctor at two in the morning. When your child gets sick, how can you tell what may be wrong? How can you be confident about calling the doctor or not? And what are the best ways of nursing your sick child safely back to good health again?

It is not usually hard to tell if your child is unwell. Any change in his normal pattern of behavior—lack of energy or a sudden loss of interest in food, for example—will put you on the alert. In addition, there are the obvious signs of illness: hot, flushed, and dry skin; unusual pallor and coldness; aches and pains; watery eyes, runny nose, or coughing; swollen glands; rashes and bumps; nausea or diarrhea. Or your child may just seem generally irritable, listless and off-color. At this stage, you may not be able to tell whether he is suffering from some minor upset or "sickening for something" more serious. So, play safe, and put him to bed or keep him quiet, away from other children, and watch how things develop.

Meanwhile, offer your child plenty of liquids —water, fruit juice, milk, or soup—as often as he wants it, but if he doesn't feel like eating, don't press him to do so. If he is vomiting or has diarrhea, stop all feeding for an hour or so to give his insides a chance to recover. Then, try offering him a teaspoonful or two of plain water. If this stays down, repeat the dose three or four times, about every 15 minutes, and then gradually increase the water to around half a glassful, sweetened with fruit juice or glucose. A jug or Thermos by the bed will save too many journeys to the kitchen. If he vomits again, go back to square one: offer him nothing for a further hour or two and gradually work your way up again. Continue with the half-glasses about once an hour until he seems better.

In general, vomiting or any other symptom that does not disappear quickly, or that tends to recur, means that you should call the doctor. After a few hours—or possibly overnight—you will probably have some idea of the nature of your child's illness. But if Billy has been ill since before lunch, or if his symptoms develop in the early evening, it is better to call the doctor then and there, rather than waiting until midnight when things seem much more desperate. From your description of the illness, the doctor will be able to decide how urgently he is needed, and he may also give you some advice on how to care for your little patient.

As a rule, say doctors, if you are seriously concerned about your child and feel you should call the doctor, then do it. Nevertheless, even experienced mothers find it reassuring to have some indication of the kind of symptoms that warrant an urgent call for medical help. Obviously any very alarming or unusual symptoms will prompt you to call your doctor immediately, but here is a checklist of some of the main symptoms that always require urgent medical attention:

1. Breathing difficulties, including croup (a rough, barking cough) with fever. And any undue coughing or hoarseness associated with breathing difficulties.

Childhood Illnesses

Disease	Incubation period*	Prevention	Symptoms	How long contagious	What you can do
Chickenpox	12–20 days, usually 14 days	None. Immune after one attack.	Mild fever followed in a day or two by rash. Successive crops of pimples appear and fill with clear fluid. Scabs form later.	7 days after rash appears, or until all scabs are dry.	Rest. Ease itching with a paste of baking soda and water, alcohol, or Calomine. Dress child in loose clothes, keep him cool, and trim fingernails to aviod scratching. Usually better in 2 weeks.
Diphtheria	2–5 days	Immunization	Sore throat, swollen neck glands, pains in limbs, foul breath. Possibly hoarseness and sharp cough. Child obviously ill.	Until laboratory tests clear.	Rest. Call doctor urgently. Follow his advice.
German measles	10–21 days, usually 18 days	Immunization	Mild fever, mild cold symptoms, rash of tiny, flat, pink spots. Glands at back of neck and behind ears may be tender and swollen.	Until rash has faded. About 4–7 days.	Moderate rest and general good care. Usually better in 4 days.
Measles	7–21 days, usually 10 days	Immunization. Gamma globulin given shortly after exposure may lessen or prevent the dissease in an unvaccinated child.	Mounting fever, runny nose, sore, red eyes, barking cough, followed in 3 to 5 days by blotchy rash starting behind ears and spreading downward.	Until rash disappears. About 10 days.	In bed for about a week on fever regime. Darkened room. Eye washes. No reading while eyes sore. Measles may be mild or severe; follow doctor's advice. Child usually feels better in 4–5 days.
Mumps	12–28 days usually 17 days	Immunization	Sometimes mild fever and headache or sore throat one day before main symptoms: swelling and ache of glands in front of ear, one side only at first. Painful to open mouth. Other parts of the body may be affected too.	Until all swelling disappears.	Moderate rest. Hot water bottle to relieve pain. Plenty of fluids. Mouth washes usually mild, especially in a young child.
Roseola	4–5 days	None. Usually affects children under 3 years, commonest under 12 months.	Sudden high fever which drops before rash, or large pink blotches appear over whole body.	Until temperature returns to normal and rash fades.	Rest and general good care.
Strep throat (septic sore throat) and scarlet fever	1–7 days, usually 2–5 days	Doctor may advise antibiotics to lessen or prevent an attack.	Possibly vomiting and fever before severe sore throat. If followed (usually in 1–4 days) by rash of tiny red spots on body and limbs, it is called scarlet fever.	Until all symptoms disappear and laboratory tests clear, or doctor agrees.	Rest and general good care. Usually cured by 10-day course of penicillin. Child will probably feel better in a week.
Whooping cough	7–21 days, usually 7–10 days	Immunization. For an unvaccinated child, protective serum may be given shortly after exposure.	Cold symptoms and cough which changes at end of second week to bouts of coughing accompanied by a noisy gasp for air (the "whoop"). Coughing often brings on vomiting. "Whoop" does not occur in babies who have the disease.	At least 4 weeks.	Rest. Soft, non-irritating foods, frequent small meals. Fresh air when doctor will allow. Breathing exercises may help. Child needs careful supervision of doctor throughout illness. Cough may continue for eight weeks.

*Usual time between exposure to disease and first symptoms.

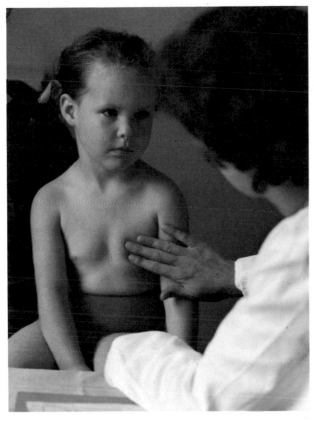

2. Nose bleeds or any other bleeding that doesn't stop within an hour.

3. Severe abdominal or any other pain that lasts for more than an hour.

4. Excessive drowsiness or loss of consciousness—when the child can't be wakened.

5. Convulsions.

6. Vomiting and diarrhea together, particularly in a baby.

7. In a baby, lack of interest in food with a weak cry or unusual quietness or apathy.

8. Emergency accidents—poisoning, bleeding that won't stop, head injury that doesn't seem better after 15 minutes, severe burns, scalds, stings, etc.

9. A sudden very high rise in temperature, if accompanied by other signs of illness.

The question of whether or not to take a child's temperature, and what a high temperature actually means, is a difficult one for mothers. A child's temperature can shoot up without anything serious being wrong, or remain near normal when the child is, in fact, quite ill. Even a healthy child's temperature doesn't stay right at 98.6° all the time—it may fluctuate between 98° and 100° and still be normal—and it naturally tends to be lower in the early morning and higher in the evening. And, of course, it is bound to be higher after a child has been running about.

To avoid unnecessary anxiety, many doctors advise that we don't really need to have a thermometer in the house. You can easily tell if your child has a fever, they say, by his appearance: flushed, dry skin, bright eyes, hot face and neck, and general listlessness. Nevertheless, there may be times when you wish to check your child's temperature and the doctor himself may sometimes suggest keeping a temperature record during the course of an illness.

A rectal thermometer is the best one to use for babies. It can register temperature in a minute or less. For a child over a year old, you may prefer to take the temperature in his armpit. This will take about four minutes to be accurate, and you can use a rectal or mouth thermometer for the job. After about the age of four, a child can usually manage safely with a mouth thermometer, but warn him not to bite it, and leave it in place for about two minutes. A rectal temperature is normally about one degree higher than a mouth temperature, and an underarm reading is likely to be one

107

degree lower, so remember to tell the doctor which method you have used.

A temperature of over 101° may mean illness, but remember once again that a high temperature is not a danger sign in itself. The important thing to note is whether the child seems sick in any way.

If your child's temperature is up to 104°, and the doctor still hasn't arrived, it is wise to try and reduce the fever a little by sponging the child—one part of the body at a time—with cool water, and to cover him only lightly with a sheet or blanket. Occasionally, a child may have a convulsion as a result of a rapid rise in temperature. If this happens, ensure that your child cannot injure himself on any sharp objects or furniture. A child who is in bed will be quite safe, although it is wise to remove his pillow. The fit will probably be over very quickly, and the child will then fall into a peaceful sleep.

What else can you do to help your child while waiting for the doctor? If your doctor has given you instructions over the phone, all well and good. Apart from following his advice, you are unlikely to need to take any urgent action before he comes. One exception, however, is in the case of difficult breathing and hoarseness or croup. This is frightening for the child, and for you. Help your child by getting him into a steam-filled atmosphere, either by using a cold steam vaporizer (a sheet draped around the sides of his crib, or an open umbrella, will help to collect the vapors), or by bringing him into the bathroom where you have run the hot shower full-on to make lots of steam. Probably the child will improve fairly rapidly, but keep the air in his room moist and stay by him until the doctor comes. (Severe croup with fever that is not helped by steaming is an emergency. If you cannot get a doctor, or he isn't already on his way to you, take the child to the nearest hospital without delay).

Most of the time, however, waiting for the doctor is simply a matter of staying with your child and mustering as much calmness as you can. Obvious anxiety on your part is likely to alarm your child more than his illness. Hard though it may be, you should do your best to

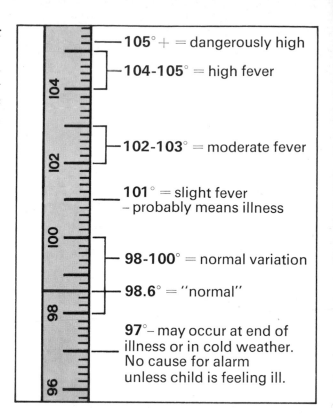

Reading a thermometer—and what those temperatures mean. Hold the thermometer so that the marks of the degrees are above and the numbers below, and roll it slightly between finger and thumb to see the mercury line. Tell the doctor the exact reading and which of the methods you used.

appear as natural and confident as possible, so that he gets the impression that you are in control and there is no need to worry. Meantime, make a mental, or even a written, note of details about your child's symptoms that might be important to the doctor. When did he start to look feverish? Has he complained of pain? When did the pain start? Did vomiting make the pain better or worse? How often did it occur? And so on. If vomit, urine, or bowel movements appear unusual in any way, it is wise to keep a sample so that your doctor can examine it.

If your child is in pain, a hot water bottle or rubbing the painful spot with a warm hand may help to soothe and comfort him. But don't give him any kind of medicine—and especially not laxatives—without the doctor's advice. If the doctor has suggested aspirin, maybe for treating fever or pain, remember to use

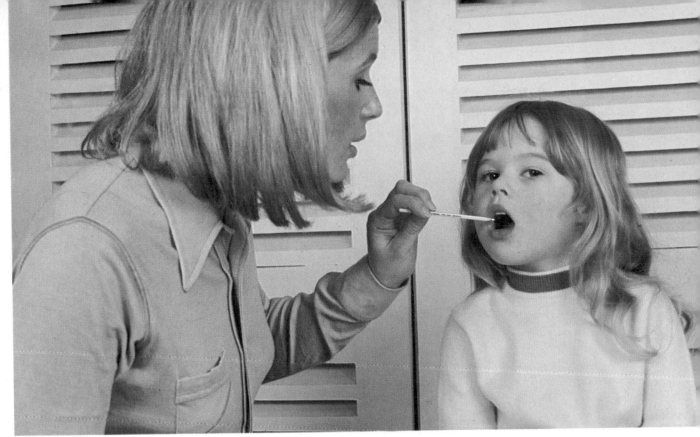

Above: taking the temperature by mouth. First, give the thermometer a few sharp shakes to drive the mercury down to 97° or less. Next, slip the thermometer bulb under the child's tongue and close her mouth. Leave the thermometer in place for 1½ to 2 minutes, and remember to wash it after use.

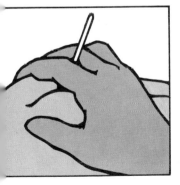

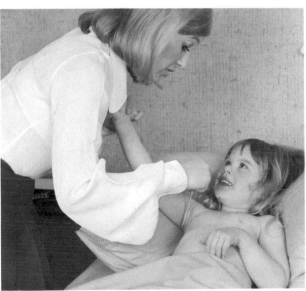

Right: taking the temperature under the arm. Hold the arm flat against the chest and wait 4 minutes. Left: taking a rectal temperature in a baby. Hold the baby across your knee, dip the thermometer bulb into petroleum jelly or cold cream, and insert gently, hold it lightly in place like this for one minute.

children's aspirin. Giving a child fractions of an adult dose of any medicine without medical advice can be dangerous.

It will be comforting for your child if you stay close while the doctor examines him, but let the child answer the doctor's questions for himself, if he is able. In non-emergencies, it is best to discuss a young child's symptoms with the doctor before he goes in to see the patient.

Hushed tones and half-heard references to his illness can be very upsetting to a child.

Fortunately, most of the illnesses children contract are minor ones. You may worry about the number of coughs, colds and other mild infections that your child gets when he first starts school, but these can usually be easily treated and your child will gradually become less susceptible to them. It is simply that he is coming into contact with new germs and his immunity to them needs time to develop. If, on the other hand, your child has prolonged bouts of being listless or unwell, it is wise to check his daily routine—enough attention, sleep, exercise, and the right diet—and to consult your doctor.

It's a sad fact that children, like grownups, may also develop symptoms due to stress. Five-year-old Peter had tummy-ache regularly every Monday morning because he was finding it hard to adapt to school life. Shy Sarah would have an attack of vomiting every time her mother planned a trip to her auntie's because she was frightened of her cousins' teasing. Six-year-old George developed a nervous twitch and started biting his nails shortly after his baby sister was born. Often, nervous symptoms like these are a necessary part of coping with temporary stress, and will pass off by themselves. If they happen frequently, however, be on the alert for any emotional problems that you may be able to relieve, with your doctor's help if necessary.

Luckily for our children, many of the once routine plagues of childhood—measles, mumps, German measles, and whooping cough—can now be prevented by immunization (see page 34). Two exceptions are chickenpox, which is usually mild in a child, and scarlet fever, once a dreaded disease but one that can now be treated quite simply and safely. Should your child be exposed to any of these diseases against which he has not been vaccinated, you should consult your doctor—in some cases, such as measles, precautionary measures may be possible.

The chart on page 106 will give you some idea of how long such an illness might take to "come out" after exposure, the symptoms to look for, what you can do to help, and how long the disease is likely to be contagious. Ideas about quarantine do, however, vary from doctor to doctor and from school to school, so you will need to check with your own doctor and your child's school for a ruling on quarantine for the patient and other members of the family.

Having a child ill is bound to be a strain for

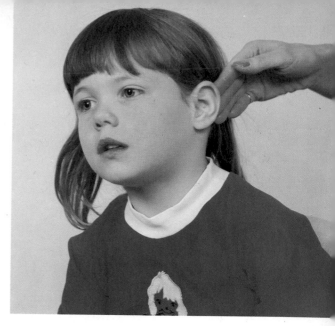

Above: examining a child's ear by pushing it gently forward. Swelling or pain may mean an infection.

Below: examine the throat by pressing gently on the tongue with the handle of a warm teaspoon.

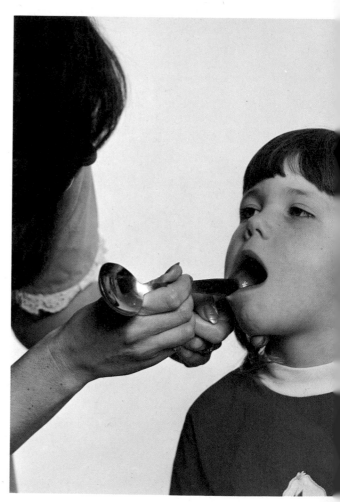

110

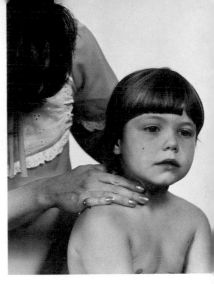

Above: when examining a child's neck, stand behind him, and have him bend his head slightly forward. That way, the neck will be relaxed, and you can feel any swellings more easily.

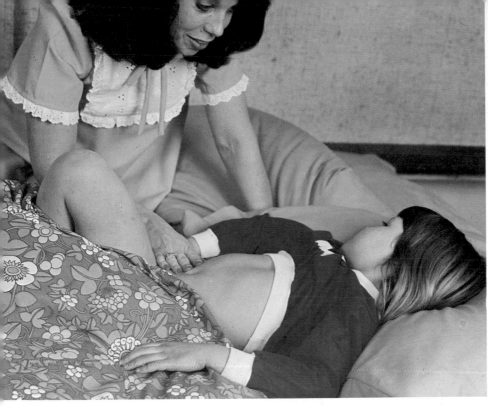

Above: examining a child with tummy-ache calls for warm and gentle hands.

Below: pains and what they may mean. (A) appendix pain usually starts here and later moves to (B). (C) liver pain. (D) pain from spleen—very rare. (E) pain here could be hernia. (F) bowel infection with diarrhea, colitis, or pain midway between a girl's periods. (G) commonest of all—minor upset.

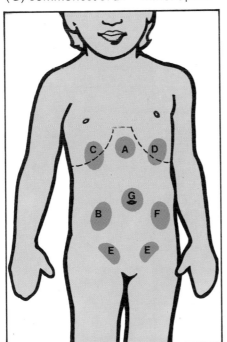

you, with all the extra work as well as the worry involved. But children recover fast from most illnesses, so there is every reason to look on the bright side and to share your optimism with your child. Medical care is safely in your doctor's hands, and he will give you advice on any special treatment. But there are lots of other ways in which you can keep your sick child cheerful and comfortable, and help him on his way to full recovery.

Bed, as most of us know, is not such a comfortable place when you have to stay there for days on end. For sitting up in bed, bolsters, or a slanting wooden board attached to the bedhead, can provide a firm foundation for pillows that would otherwise slide down into the bed. An adjustable table that can be swung across the bed is ideal for games and toys. Or you could make a makeshift bed table by placing a board across the bed supported on the backs of two upright chairs. Toys could be stored in a pillowcase or shopping bag tied to the bed, or in a drawer or cardboard box at bed level. And pencils will always be on hand if you tie them to the bedhead with string.

A good way to prevent small toys and crumbs from finding their way into the bed is to tie a large sheet (ribbons at the corners will

111

Amusing Your Sick Child

Age	Companionship	Useful toys	Occupations	Games
1–4 +	Soft toys, doll to dress and undress, toy telephone.	Bricks, large, simple jigsaws, fitting pictures, plastic cups and other fitting-together toys, doll's house, toy cars.	Picture books, cutting out, drawing, coloring, large beads and buttons for threading.	Nursery rhymes, stories, fantasy games.
4–8 +	Soft toys, small mobile toys, hand puppets, pets, bird, aquarium, radio, record player.	Bricks, jigsaws, model-making, mosaics, easy constructional toys, miniature garages, farms, zoos, toy cars.	Reading, drawing, painting, stencilling, modeling clay, sewing, weaving, knitting, cutting out, making scrapbooks.	Guessing games, simple card games, playing out the illness, doctor and nurse sets.
8–11 +	Soft toys, pets, bird, hamster, fish, puppets, Solitaire, card games, radio, record player.	Jigsaws, model-making, construction sets.	Reading, writing, painting, sewing, weaving, soft toy making, basket-making, theater.	Doctor and nurse sets, board games.
11 and upward	Pets, puppets, Solitaire, card games, radio, record player.	Jigsaws, model-, toy-, and jewelry-making, complicated construction sets.	Reading, painting, carving, sewing, and other crafts, making a miniature garden, collecting stamps, badges, photos, etc.	Play-reading, word games, crosswords, board and card games.

Books, paper, and pencils for all ages.

Above: in case you should run short of ideas, these suggestions may help you come up with some games and play to keep your young convalescent amused.

Right: some children will happily spend long periods reading when they start to get well, but other toys should be on hand at the bedside.

help) around your child's waist and tuck it well under the mattress at each side. If you use waterproof sheeting, the bedcovers will stay clean, too, and your child will be able to play happily with paints and modeling clay without getting everything in a mess. He will probably feel more comfortable, too, if you let him wear his ordinary clothes during the day. A pullover, underpants, and socks are less likely to get tangled than a nightie or pyjamas, and a change of clothes before sleep will be refreshing. Moving his bed close to the window will give him something to look at when he is bored, and you could cheer up his room with flowers and plants, or pin different pictures on the walls from day to day.

Provided the doctor agrees, it is better to let your child get up, at least for part of the day, rather than staying miserably cooped up in bed.

Make up a bed on the living room sofa, if necessary, so that he can be close to you and the rest of the family. This applies to adult invalids, too. Sick people feel better, and get better more quickly, if there is activity going on around them and they can share, even a little, in normal day-to-day life. However, you will need to keep an eye out to see that your young invalid doesn't get overtired by playing for more than short periods with healthy brothers and sisters.

If your child must stay in bed, try to make sure he still feels "one of the family" by including him as much as you can in home life, and letting brothers and sisters, or little friends, pay regular, short visits (unless, of course, his illness is contagious). See how many of your activities you could move into the sickroom—sewing, mending, ironing, peeling the vegetables, or sharing a meal. Pets, too, could come to call regularly, and fish, a hamster, or a bird would make ideal long-term companions.

A sick child will thrive best on a regular routine for washing, eating, playing, and resting, and this can be a boon in planning your day. Start the morning with a cool drink and a refreshing wash before breakfast. Your doctor will have advised you if your child needs a special diet. Otherwise, light foods, such as toast, cereal, crackers, cookies, soup, custards, junket, stewed fruit, and ice cream, will be the most he can manage at first. If he does not feel like eating at all, don't let this worry you, but continue to offer him plenty of fruit juice and sweetened drinks throughout the day. Milk is fine, if he can take it, and skimmed milk will be easier to digest. Later, as he begins to get better, you could start gradually reintroducing nourishing, easy-to-eat foods like eggs, fish, and ground meat, as well as fruit and vegetables.

Even when a child is convalescing, however, he may still not show much interest in food. This is not just because of his illness, but because he is not getting much exercise and is

using up less energy than usual. It is best to let his appetite be your guide to how much food he needs. Urging him to eat, or fussing over his appetite, could cause feeding problems that last long after his illness is over. But of course you are anxious to see him eating well again, and it will help a lot if you stick to the foods you know he likes and try to make his meals look as attractive as possible. Small amounts of food with contrasting colors, or a prettily laid tray with a colorful napkin, may take a little extra trouble but are well worth trying. An individual portion of meat loaf in its own little dish, or tiny servings of various foods in lots of small containers (such as cupcake holders or dishes made from foil) will look more tempting than a substantial plateful of food. Try serving drinks in his favorite mug—perhaps with colored straws—or treat him to a special new one. Having small helpings of whatever the rest of the family is eating often encourages an invalid to eat. It's best not to ask him in advance what he would like for dinner, or he will have time to lose his capricious appetite and that specially-prepared meal may go to waste. In general, aim to provide frequent small meals, with no eating in between—and don't forget about teeth-cleaning before he goes to sleep.

Encouraging your child to eat may seem simple compared with getting him to take his medicine. But "medicine time" doesn't have to be a tearful battle of wits. The best approach is to be as relaxed and matter-of-fact about the whole thing as you can. Take it for granted that Johnny will swallow his medicine and just pop it into his mouth while you chat about something else. Many medicines for children are pleasantly flavored, but in case it is not, have a glass of water, a slice of orange, or a candy on hand to take away the taste afterwards.

Whole or crushed tablets will go down more easily in a teaspoonful of mashed banana or honey. Or you could try mixing crushed tablets in a little glucose water, syrup, or fruit juice. Choose a drink that is different from his regular milk or juice—he may get to dislike old favorites that suddenly develop a peculiar taste.

If you use the smallest possible amount of liquid, your child is more likely to take it all, and less powder will cling to the side of the cup.

If you know that medicine is going to taste horrible anyway, it is best to be honest about it. "I know it's nasty, but it will help you get better, and I'll hold your hand while you take it," is kinder than suggesting he won't get better unless he has it. Above all, steer clear of hinting that if he is a good boy he won't need to have any more horrid medicine—when you know there is half a bottleful still to come.

One thing your sick child does need is a big dose of you. Doctors say that a child who is sick becomes at least a year younger mentally than when he is well. He is likely to revert to more babyish habits, to be more dependent, and to need more direct signs of affection So go right ahead and give him all the extra cuddling and cosseting you like. Spoiling doesn't come into it when a child is really ill. Once he starts to get better, however, it is wise to encourage him gently but firmly to return to his ordinary routine, so that he won't get too attached to the privileges of being pampered.

Anyone who has ever been ill knows how the days can drag. And a child can feel very lonely and isolated up there in his room. Ideally he shouldn't be left alone for longer than about 20 minutes at a time. But when you are too busy to manage such frequent visits, it will help to let him know you're around if he can hear you going about your work. The clatter of pots and pans, the whirr of the vacuum cleaner, the sound of your voice, singing, humming, or even thinking aloud, will all be comforting evidence that Mommy isn't far away and all is well. He will need to be able to call you, too, of course, and here a bell or a toy drum can be useful. If you can resign yourself to some needless ringing and banging at first, you will probably be able to agree on a simple code to signal essential requests. Alternatively, a baby alarm can be the perfect answer to communication problems.

When you do go in to see the invalid, try to make a little time for a proper visit, rather than dashing in and out just to check that he is all right. A cheerful chat about what you are

Right: even when a young invalid is up and about, he still needs lots of company. It helps if you can set aside regular times to play with him, or let him feel he is sharing your activities as a full-time member of the family again.

Below: with a little encouragement from mother, medicine time need not be a battle. If she treats the whole thing lightly, so will he, and some fruit or a candy afterward will help take away the nasty taste.

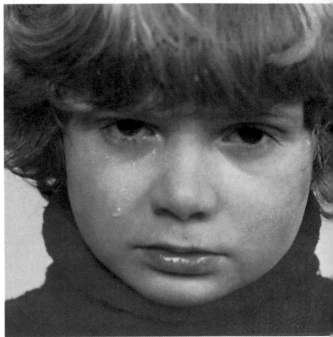

doing, or sharing in a game will be more comforting than too many questions about the progress of his symptoms. A clock in the bedroom might help, even for a younger child. If you can promise to be back "when the big hand gets to four," he will probably be happier about letting you go.

Father's visits are important, too. A lot of insecurity goes with being ill, and the child needs to know that Daddy is just as concerned about him as Mommy. All too often, of course, fathers have the peachiest role in caring for sick children. They're the ones who arrive with special presents and pampering for half-an-hour before it's time for sleep. And while Daddy's goodnight story or game is an important high spot in a sick child's day, it is a good idea to share some of the less pleasant tasks of nursing with your husband, too, so that you don't become the sole giver of foul medicines and firm orders.

Once your child is over the worst phase of his illness, he is likely to become crotchety, demanding—and bored. Take heart! This is trying, but it is a good sign. It means he is getting better. But how, oh how, do you keep a restless, bedbound child amused, or cope with the convalescent who hangs onto the furniture and whines that he's bored?

One of the reasons a convalescent gets so peevish is that, in spite of his returning energy, he tires easily and can't concentrate for long. So variety is the keynote in keeping him amused. That doesn't mean spending a fortune on an endless supply of new toys. All his familiar treasures will be welcome, and very often a sick child will prefer the battered old rabbit or favorite storybook he outgrew last

Left: tears come easily to the child who has not yet recovered the energy for all the things he would like to be doing.

Right: bouts of irritability and peevishness during convalescence call for lots of patient understanding from mother.

year to any smart new plaything. The trick is to give him only a few toys at a time—say, one to play with and two or three extras by his bed—and to take them away once he has finished playing with them. That way, the same toys can make a triumphant comeback later. Intersperse his old favorites with some inexpensive new playthings, bearing in mind that he will need simpler games than usual and toys that are easy to handle.

A toddler will go for soft, cuddly toys, building bricks, fitting-together toys, and toys that make a noise—even his old rattle could be welcome. He may like dolls that can be dressed and undressed, a toy telephone, or a brightly colored picture book that he can tear up. He will enjoy having you read him stories, sing him nursery rhymes, help him with a simple jigsaw, draw for him, or make boats and funny

hats out of paper. An older toddler can get lots of amusement from paper and crayons, coloring books, modelling clay, stringing large beads or buttons, and blowing soap bubbles. He could use a pair of blunt scissors to cut pictures out of old magazines or Christmas cards, but he will need your help pasting them into a scrapbook.

Scrapbooks are popular with older children, too, and they may like to make their own books, greeting cards, or even a pictorial dictionary. They will also enjoy drawing, painting, and stencilling, playing records, making mosaics, knitting, and even sorting out your sewing box. Toys that are popular with 5 to 8 year-olds are jigsaws, constructional sets, model-making, and puppets. Over-8's will like these, too, and they will probably be interested in weaving sets, pegboards, model theaters,

117

Back out-of-doors with his favorite friend, and brimming over with good health again, the little invalid has already forgotten all about those long tiresome days he spent being cooped up ill in bed.

card and dice games. At this age, books are a boon, and your child will probably enjoy writing—particularly sending and receiving letters. Budding teenagers will be happiest with simpler versions of adult activities—collecting coins, stamps, badges, or photos, carving, sewing, making toys or jewellery, doing crossword puzzles, reading, listening to the radio, or making a miniature garden.

Television is, of course, popular with all age-groups, and it does help to keep a sick child amused—in small doses. It is not wise to make the TV your babysitter by leaving your child alone with it for long stretches. And remember to check beforehand on the programs he is to watch. Violent or over-exciting movies, for example, could be especially distressing for a sick child. Throughout the day, try to alternate passive and active occupations, and share his play, at least to start him off. The happiest way will probably be to set aside regular times when you will read to him, play with him, or think up a new game. Unless his illness is a particularly long one, don't worry about the school he is missing and try to give him lessons. He can't cope with these while he is ill, and his toys and games will be education enough for the time being.

Above all, be truthful with your child about his illness. When he asks, "When will I be better?" "When can I go out and play?" give him an honest answer. Maybe you'll just have to say, "As soon as we can get you better," or pass the question on to your doctor, who is an expert at tactful replies. But, in the case of most childhood illnesses, you will probably be able to say "very soon," or "next week," and mean it, because it really won't be long before your child is up and about and his healthy self again.

118

Looking After Yourself

8

Many of women's traditional roles may be changing, but the fact is that everyone still turns to mother to keep things running smoothly in the home. So how can you make sure that they do? How do you cope with the housework and the family, and maybe with someone who's ill—and still find time to take care of your own health, not to mention your sanity?

When it's a question of priorities, we tend to put ourselves last. But it is vital to pay as much attention to your own well-being as to that of your family. You need regular, well-balanced meals, sufficient exercise, sleep, and relaxation just as much as they do. And, after all, if you neglect your own health, you will be neglecting your family, too, simply because they do depend on you so much.

How often, for example, can any of us be bothered to cook for ourselves in the middle of the day? All too often, during the early morning rush you may be too busy to have breakfast, and just snatch a cup of coffee when the family has left for school or work. And if the kids' lunch of peanut butter sandwiches and soup doesn't appeal to you, you may make do with yet another coffee and a few cookies. That leaves you having to pack all your nutritional requirements into one meal in the evening. And it isn't enough. So how about keeping some good and nutritious "snackables" around for yourself—hard-boiled eggs, cheese, cold meat, tomatoes, yoghurt, and fruit? And why not have some of these for breakfast? There's no rule that says cheese or ham are only for lunch—in fact they are standard breakfast fare in some countries—and such foods are quick and easy to eat as well as being nutritious.

Cold foods are just as good for you as hot ones. In fact, raw fruits and vegetables are *more* nutritious because some of their vitamins are lost in cooking. So if time is short, or your day has been thrown out of gear, try giving the family a cold meal for a change. Other times, you might be able to prepare food ahead and make double quantities—it takes no longer and will cut down on cooking time later in the week. Make full use of your automatic timer if your stove has one. And remember, small sizes cook quicker. If you're in a rush, cut vegetables small before cooking.

How about exercise? You are probably getting a fair amount of that by working around the house. But that may mean using the same muscles over and over again, while the others don't get their fair share of activity. If you can get out for a walk on your own during the day, you will be getting valuable exercise and fresh air, as well as having a peaceful few moments to yourself. But even if solo jaunts are out, taking your toddler to the park to play, or walking a young child to school can be good exercise, too.

Muscles can be tense without our realizing it and can make us less efficient and more accident-prone, as well as causing aches and pains. Try to fit in a couple of relaxing exercises, or brief rest periods, at your least busy times of day—when the family has left in the morning, or after lunch, for example. Here is just one soothing exercise to try. Lying flat on the couch or floor, contract the muscles of your

In the busy round of caring for a home and family, and maybe having an outside job as well, a woman can all too easily underrate the importance of looking after her own health and well-being, too.

leg as hard as you can, and then let them go again until they feel so limp that you are only conscious of their weight on the floor. Repeat the same exercise with each set of muscles in turn—legs, body, arms, jaw, and face—allowing your eyelids to open a little as you breathe in and to close very slowly as you breathe out, and concentrating on the sensation of weight as your muscles relax. After a bit of practice at this kind of exercise, you may find that you don't even need to lie down to do it, and you can use the same basic method to relax various sets of muscles while you are doing routine household jobs, standing in line at the supermarket, or waiting for a bus. Yoga exercises are also good ones to try, and so are the relaxation exercises you may have learned during pregnancy. Such exercises have been found particularly valuable in relieving the kind of tension that may cause headaches, abdominal pain, or backache. Controlled breathing is also a great aid to relaxation. Begin by exhaling as deeply as you can. That way, you will automatically take in a deeper breath, too, and you can then continue with a regular rhythm of slow, even breathing.

Just as your husband needs a complete change from the problems of work to relieve stress, you need a rest from the children now and again, in order to relax and renew your energies. An evening out with your husband, with friends, or following some particular interest of your own, or an occasional weekend without the kids, will do you a lot of good, and help you appreciate the children more when you get back. Give vacations high priority in your budget, too, for the sake of your—and your family's—health. Try to ensure that you always have an annual break away

from home—provided, of course, that doesn't mean cooking and cleaning in a holiday house instead of your own home.

You can do a lot to spread yourself around—and find time for yourself—if you look for ways of organizing your life to save time and energy. Try sharing jobs around the family a bit more. Children can enjoy the responsibility of sharing family tasks, and this may teach them self-discipline as well as useful skills. How many wives today wish their husbands had learned something about helping around the house when they were children?

The best way to assign tasks is through a family conference. A rotation system could

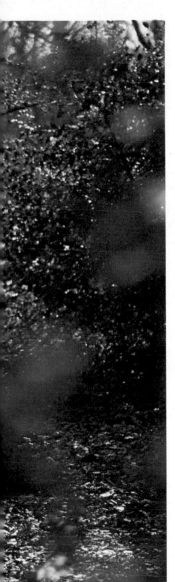

Left: a walk with your child can be one easy way of getting some valuable fresh air and exercise.

Below: everyone needs a break from routine to help them stay fit. A vacation, however short, should be high on a family's list of priorities.

appeal to a child's sense of justice, and avoid arguments about whose turn it is to do what, but bear in mind each child's particular skills and interests, and give him the chance to volunteer for the jobs he prefers. Can Bobby make the beds and keep his own room tidy? Is Andrew an expert polisher? Does Sally enjoy using the washing machine? Remember to give plenty of praise for a job well done. A hug or a warm "thank you" is better than offering extra pocket-money for household tasks. After all, such tasks are part of family sharing, and can teach your child about the value of mutual helpfulness within the family.

That word "mutual" is important. A child will be more willing to help if you offer to help him, too, sometimes, and if he sees his father and mother sharing tasks in the home. Can your husband look after getting the kids bathed and into bed in the evening? Or do the dinner dishes, and the final evening clear-up? If TV and the evening newspaper are all he's ready for after work, how about asking him to take over more of the weekend duties—shopping, fixing breakfast, and so on? If he's a confirmed non-helper, it might help to remind him of that survey which calculated that the average housewife performs around 12 specialized functions for 99.6 hours a week (if she were paid for these, she should be getting a salary

The household load can be lightened when members of the family are all willing to lend a hand. Children may like the responsibility of sharing family tasks, and they can learn a lot about co-operation if they see Dad and Mom both doing their bit to help each other out—with a smile, too.

of over $10,000 a year). That means that your working hours are more than twice as long as your husband's. Can you maybe sit down together and work out some fairer apportionment of time, tasks, and family funds?

Trying to keep the house spotless, day-in, day-out, is an impossible task when there are kids around. So try not to set your standards too high, or worry about the opinions of others. Put the family—and yourself—first. Families don't need clinically clean homes to be happy. Can you leave things sometimes? You know you won't be able to get everything done, and worrying about it just wastes precious time and energy. Most busy career wives and mothers agree that the only way to cope is to get used to doing only what needs to be done *now*.

A certain amount of routine —getting up in good time to start the day more relaxed, regular mealtimes, certain days for regular, big chores —can help keep things under control, provided it is not so strict as to become thoroughly boring or over-dominate your life. Make work easier, too, by using labor-saving equipment in the areas where you most need it and by taking short-cuts where you can. Try using quick-cleaners for oven, floors, and windows, choose easy-care furnishing materials, shop when the stores are least busy. Keep some cleaning things upstairs as well as down, and use carts and trays for quick tidying-up. Soak pans right after use to make them easier to wash later, and find out the best method of using kitchen equipment or cleaning materials—this can save mishaps as well as time.

Whatever their job, most people find that the best way to avoid getting overwhelmed by the sheer amount of work to be done is to con-

centrate on getting through it bit by bit. And it's important to know when to stop, says one doctor. Just a ten-minute break can be refreshing if you take it when you first feel tired. Go on pushing yourself until you are thoroughly exhausted and even a couple of hours' rest won't do you half as much good. Try splitting up the day's workload into a series of mini-tasks, so that you can get some feeling of satisfaction when you finish each one. Plan little oases in a day that is filled with a seemingly endless round of routine tasks. Promise yourself some kind of reward after each particular job—an apple, a cup of coffee, calling a friend, taking a short walk, or spending ten minutes with your feet up.

Of course, there are some days when nothing seems to go right. And there is no sure-fire way of side-stepping life's minor irritations. Some we can dodge by a bit of reorganization —by putting bills in a special folder rather than tossing them aside to disappear without trace, by making one night a week bill-paying, or letter-writing, night, by checking cupboards and making a list before doing the marketing, or by getting up just that little bit earlier. Against others, the only weapon is to cultivate a sense of humor. "If you don't take yourself too seriously," says one busy mother, "no one and nothing will upset you for long."

It is generally agreed that one of the best ways of combating everyday stresses, and of insulating ourselves against feelings of depression, loneliness, or dissatisfaction, is to seek the kind of outside activities that will help us lead fuller and more interesting lives. This may mean a tremendous initial effort to decide what we want to do, to overcome fears of possible failure, and to get out and do it. But by committing ourselves to developing some talent that has previously gone unused or to learning new skills, by participating in group activities, or by working to help others, we may strengthen our confidence in our own worth, as well as finding life richer and more rewarding.

On the other hand, of course, we may sometimes get ourselves overcommitted. Are you always the one relied on to arrange coffee parties, organize child-minding, or fund-raising? It's possible to be too kind-hearted and then to resent it when others impose too greatly on your willingness to help. It's important to know when to say no, and to be brave enough to refuse when such demands begin to encroach too heavily on your time and your personal life.

Setting priorities is a problem for every mother. Her husband needs her, her children need her, she has to run her home, maybe she has an outside job as well—and she needs time for herself. While it is flattering to be needed so much, dealing with family members whose ages may range from 8 days to 80 years, and coping with a multitude of daily tasks, without ever neglecting one for the other, can make any woman feel like bottom acrobat in a circus balancing act. But there are ways of making your family feel loved even if you can't be there. Can you leave a note to welcome Suzie home from school if you have to be out with Henry at the dentist? Could you visit your mother by telephone this week if one of the children is sick? How about planning a family treat to celebrate when you finally finish those curtains you have been making, or when Billy gets to be captain of his ball team? Or saving up some of the funny events of the day to make the rest of the family laugh over dinner?

Mother's moods have an uncanny knack of rubbing off on the rest of the family. It seems unfair that, when you are grouchy, they are bad-tempered too. But that doesn't mean you have to make a superhuman effort to be cheerful when you are feeling low. Far better to be honest and say you're blue, especially if you can explain some of the reasons why. Similarly, there is no point in struggling heroically through your work with 102° of fever. No one needs a martyr for a mother, and you'll only make them miserable worrying about you. If you don't feel well, do what you'd advise them to do—rest up and see your doctor, if necessary.

The same reasoning applies when you're the nurse. We all know that, when a child gets sick, there is no one in the world he wants more than Mommy. But if you are to go on being patient and sympathetic, you need some help, too. Often, at least some of the extra work can be shared within the family. But if a child—or any other member of the family—is going to need nursing for any length of time, you might like to consider having a relative to stay and help. Are there neighbors who could lend a hand with shopping, or sit in for 15 minutes each day while you get a little fresh air and exercise? If things really become too much, don't struggle on unaided. Consult your local health department about outside help. Find out about voluntary or home-help services in your community. And, of course, if friends volunteer to help, don't wait to be asked twice. By looking after your own health and well-being, as well as your family's, you will be ensuring that they get the best possible care from a mother who recognizes just how important she is to those who love her most.

126

Questions & Answers

Your child falls on his head. How can you tell if he is seriously hurt? What should you do before calling the doctor? Your husband collapses with pain in his chest. Is it a heart attack? Should you bundle him into the car and rush him to hospital? An unconscious person could die if you leave him lying on his back? Why? Is thrusting a burned arm under cold water the right thing to do? Your child has swallowed sleeping tablets. Should you immediately make him vomit? Is there time to call the doctor?

When a serious accident or sudden illness happens, you must know what to do *at once*. There is no time to thumb frantically through a first aid manual. There may not even be time to call for medical help. You have to act instantly—and you have to do the right thing. That means knowing in advance the kind of action to take. The following pages will help to give you that advance knowledge in a way that is easy to read and to remember. Here is straightforward, practical advice on handling some of the commonest and most dangerous emergencies that any one of us might have to face at some time in our lives: bleeding, shock, stopped breathing, falls, fractures and head injuries, burns and scalds, poisoning, unconsciousness and fainting, heart attack and stroke.

Maybe you think that reading about first-aid won't do any good. Maybe you feel you are bound to forget all you ever read in the panic of a crisis. Can reading about first aid really help you to cope in an emergency? Yes, it can —provided the information tells you *why* to do things, as well as *how*. The advice you will read here includes clear explanations of the whys and wherefores of any action to be taken. These pages tell you what symptoms you will see when someone suffers an accident, what those symptoms mean, the specific dangers entailed, and how, because of this, you should deal with them. They will give you the basic information that you can apply in any major emergency. These pages will take you maybe 15 minutes to read. In 15 minutes, you could know how to save a life—maybe the life of someone very dear and close to you.

Knowing how best to look after your family's health, and protect them from danger or illness, gives you a confidence they know they can trust.

Bleeding

How much blood do we have in our bodies?

The average adult has about five to six quarts of blood, flowing through some 60,000 miles of blood vessels. The blood makes a complete journey round the body about once a minute, carrying water and oxygen to all the cells and collecting waste products from them, circulating hormones, and distributing antibodies to fight infection.

Does a big person have more blood than a small one?

Yes. We have about one pint of blood for every 12 pounds of body weight. And for every excess pound of weight we gain, the body has to build an extra mile of blood vessels—another sobering thought for the overweight!

Blood donors give about a pint of blood without ill effects. Yet the same amount of blood pouring from a wound seems pretty serious. How much blood can we lose without danger?

The average person can lose a pint of blood without danger, and that is why this is the amount usually chosen for blood donating. However, the loss of blood from a wound should always be taken seriously. At a blood donating center, a pint of blood is given under carefully controlled conditions. In the case of accidental bleeding, not only would it be hard to judge the amount of blood being lost, but there is the added risk of infection from germs that may enter a wound. It has been shown that the body *can* lose up to a third of its blood supply (about four pints for the average person) without apparent serious effect, but the loss of half the body's blood is almost always fatal, and even the loss of two pints of blood will often cause shock (see page 132).

What should I do if someone is bleeding badly?

First, stop the bleeding. Then summon medical help. If someone else can call an ambulance while you deal with the bleeding, so much the better. To stop heavy bleeding, immediately press your fingers, or the palm of your hand, directly on the bleeding area, using a clean cloth if possible. Press the edges of the wound firmly together, and continue pressing with your hand until the bleeding has abated. Don't waste time looking for bandages. Grab the cleanest material at hand—a towel, a shirt, a clean handkerchief—to use as a pad. If you have no material of any kind, just press on the wound with your bare fingers. The hospital will be able to take care of cleaning the wound later. While maintaining firm and constant pressure on the wound, seat or lay the casualty down, preferably with his legs raised, and raise the bleeding part, if possible, to reduce the flow of blood. When blood soaks through the original pad, don't remove the pad, but cover it as fast as possible with new layers of material. (Removing the pad would disturb any blood clot forming in the wound, and could make bleeding worse.) When the bleeding eases up, secure the pads firmly with a bandage or strips of cloth until you can get medical help. Remember, heavy loss of blood may cause dangerous shock, so, having stopped the bleeding, the casualty must be got to the hospital urgently.

What if the bleeding just won't stop?

Even the most severe and profuse bleeding can almost always be stopped by direct, continued pressure. If the bleeding does not abate, you are probably not pressing in the right place, so shift your pressing fingers until you hit on the right spot. Several minutes of this firm pressure should be enough to control the bleeding sufficiently for a thick, firm dressing (a makeshift one if need be) to be applied. If bleeding still continues as profusely as ever when you take your fingers away, you must just keep on pressing until you can get the casualty to the hospital.

Shouldn't I use a tourniquet?

No. A tourniquet, if wrongly applied, can be extremely dangerous and cause more harm than the injury itself. A tourniquet, or constrictive bandage, stops bleeding by cutting off the blood supply to an injured arm or leg, but if it is put on too tightly and not loosened often enough, it may cause the entire limb to die. A tourniquet should therefore never be used except by a trained person, and even then, is rarely necessary. Applying direct pressure on to the wound by fingers or hand is usually just as effective and far safer.

What about a bullet wound?

A bullet wound may be superficial or involve internal bleeding and serious damage. Stop heavy bleeding by direct pressure until help arrives. Cover a surface wound with sterile gauze, but don't try to clean it until you have received medical advice. If the wound is internal, check for breathing and give mouth-to-mouth resusciatation if necessary. Keep the patient lying down, with his head low if possible, to aid the supply of blood to the brain. Wrap coats or blankets under and over his body, and call an ambulance urgently.

How can I tell if internal bleeding has occurred after an injury?

Internal bleeding may occur in the chest, abdomen, or skull, following a fall, blow, crash, or injury from a stab or bullet. It can also happen in certain chest or abdominal illnesses. The bleeding may remain unseen, or blood may escape from the body sometime after the injury. Symptoms of internal bleeding may include shock, dizziness, loss of consciousness, pallor, rapid breathing, severe pain or swelling, and anxiety. If you suspect internal bleeding, do not move the patient. Keep him lying down, warmly covered, with his head low, and send for urgent medical help.

What is the best treatment for just a small cut or scratch?

Wash the cut under cold running water, and cleanse the surrounding skin with soap and water, remembering to wipe *away* from the wound edges. Pat it dry with a sterile gauze pad, and cover it with a small bandage to prevent infection.

I notice you don't mention applying anti-septic. Isn't this essential?

No. While it is important to prevent harmful bacteria from entering a cut where they may cause infection, most doctors agree that ordinary soap and water are sufficient to remove these bacteria from the skin, and any germs that do enter a small wound will probably be killed more effectively by the body s natural defenses than by an antiseptic. If you do wish to use an antiseptic, doctors say, choose isopropyl (rubbing) alcohol—it is just as effective as any other antiseptic and is less likely to cause an allergic reaction. Be sure to apply it to the skin *around* the wound, rather than on the wound itself. The body naturally sheds dirt and germs to the surface of a wound, and any antiseptic applied directly to a wound may seal germs in rather than keeping them out. In the case of a large or deep wound there is, of course, a much greater risk of infection, and such wounds should always be treated by a doctor.

When is an anti-tetanus injection needed after a wound?

Tetanus (sometimes called *lockjaw* because it causes spasms of the jaw) is a very serious infection that can be fatal. It is caused by organisms that live in the large intestines of most domestic animals. These organisms pass out with the excreta of such animals and go on living for a long time in dirt, soil, or street dust. If a wound is contaminated by such dirt or soil, some of these organisms may get into the body. Particularly hazardous are so-called *puncture wounds,* from, say, a rusty nail or a dog bite, which may cause little bleeding but go deep under the skin. Because children are so likely to suffer minor cuts and scrapes while playing, it is standard practice to immunize children against tetanus during their first year and every few years thereafter. If, however, your child suffers a puncture wound, or any other wound from a object that has been lying in the dirt or out of doors, you should ask your doctor to give the child a booster injection if he has not had a shot for one year. If the victim is an adult, ask a doctor whether an anti-tetanus inoculation is necessary.

Shock

What is shock?

Shock is a dangerous state of collapse, which, if not controlled, can be fatal.

What causes shock?

Shock occurs when the supply of blood to the brain is reduced to such an extent that the brain cannot operate efficiently, and the vital body functions that it controls are disrupted. Shock may therefore arise in any condition that upsets the circulation of the blood, such as heavy loss of blood or body fluids (as in serious injuries, large fractures, and burns); internal bleeding from a burst appendix or perforated ulcer; heart attack, or stroke. If the blood supply to the brain is cut off entirely, the brain cannot survive for long, and the person may easily die.

How can I tell if someone is suffering from shock?

When a person goes into shock, he may feel giddy and nauseous, grow extremely pale, and perspire profusely. His skin may be cold and clammy, his vision blurred, and his breathing rapid but shallow. He may complain of thirst, become restless and anxious, and possibly lose consciousness. However, the vital thing to remember is that shock is likely to occur in any serious medical emergency and should be treated urgently without waiting for specific symptoms to appear.

How should shock be treated?

Stop any bleeding by direct pressure and call urgently for medical help. Remember, shock is caused by a shortage of blood to the brain, and without blood the brain cannot function for long. Treatment must therefore be directed toward restoring the blood supply to the brain as quickly as possible. In the case of heavy bleeding or loss of body fluid, medical treatment will probably involve a transfusion to replace the blood or fluid lost. That is why it is vital to get the patient to hospital as fast as possible even when bleeding has been stemmed.

While waiting for an ambulance to arrive, keep the patient quiet, comfortable, and reassured. Above all, keep his head low, so that blood can reach the brain more easily. If possible, arrange the patient so that he is lying down with his legs raised (on pillows, cushions, or folded coats) and his head turned to one side in case he vomits. If he is unconscious, use the coma position (see page 141). Loosen any tight clothing and cover him with a blanket or coat. Keep the room warm, but do not overheat the patient or use a hot water bottle to warm him. The heat from this will divert blood away from the brain, where it is vitally needed, to the skin, where it is not. Give nothing to eat or drink, except to a *conscious* burned casualty (see page 138).

Won't alcohol or a warm drink help?

No. On the contrary, such drinks may be positively harmful. The heat from a warm drink, just like that of a hot-water bottle, will tend to divert much-needed blood away from the brain to other parts of the body. Alcohol, too, causes the blood vessels in the skin to open up and carry more blood to the skin (that is what produces the familiar feeling of warmth we experience after a drink). Unconscious casualties could choke to death if forced to drink. Those with chest, abdominal, or internal injuries could be further injured. And many casualties will need an anesthetic after arrival in hospital, for which it is necessary to have an empty stomach. Even burn victims, who need fluids, should be given only *cool* water drinks.

Can't a sudden fright or hearing very bad news cause shock? Does this have the same dangerous effect on the body?

True shock is always caused by a serious shortage of blood supply to the brain, usually due to the kind of emergencies we have been talking about. However, severe fright, extreme pain, a horrifying sight, or other violent emotional experience can cause a kind of shock. Known as *nerve shock,* this usually causes fainting, due to an impairment of the nervous system, but it may result in many of the symptoms of shock already described. In nerve shock, blood tends to pool in the blood vessels, so that there is less blood available for general circulation. The big difference between this kind of emotional shock and serious physical shock, however, is that nerve shock can almost always be quickly and simply relieved by treating the patient for fainting (see page 141). In this case, too, it will do no harm to give the patient a warm, sweetened drink—but not alcohol—*once he is conscious and has started to recover*. However, it is vital to remember that these measures apply *only* where the cause of shock is purely emotional, and can be dangerously time-wasting if the patient is suffering from true shock following some medical emergency.

Resuscitation

How long can a person live without breathing?

Probably for only four to six minutes. The air we breathe in supplies the oxygen that is vital to keep every part of the body alive. And the brain, which itself controls breathing, is the first to suffer from lack of oxygen. If no air is entering the lungs, the heart will continue to beat for a little longer, supplying blood to the brain and other parts of the body. But soon, the supply of oxygen already in the blood is used up. First, the patient loses consciousness, because the brain is no longer getting sufficient oxygen to function. Then lack of oxygen in the heart causes it to stop beating. Without oxygen, the brain can survive undamaged for only about four minutes. The heart may survive for as long as 12 minutes. But within six minutes, the person will almost certainly be dead.

What do I do if someone stops breathing?

Anyone who is with you should immediately summon emergency aid, but don't waste a second shifting the patient or calling for help yourself. Your one aim is to get air into his body as fast as possible, and you have three priorities: make sure his air passages are clear; breathe air into his lungs; and stimulate his heart if it has stopped beating. *In a baby or*

small child who has been choking or gasping for breath before becoming unconscious, the air passage is probably blocked by some object stuck in his throat, so immediately hold the child up by the heels, or over your lap with his head down, and slap his back sharply several times. This alone will probably be enough to dislodge the object and enable breathing to start again. *In an adult*, clear the air passage by bending the patient's head back as far as it will go, pressing firmly on the forehead or pulling on his hair. At the same time, push the lower jaw upward and forward until the teeth meet. (Don't be afraid to pull the head really well back—it is surprising just how far back the neck can stretch). In this position, the tongue cannot fall back and block the back of the throat and that may be the only reason why an unconscious person cannot breathe. He may now gasp and start breathing. If not, quickly check the inside of his mouth for any other obstructions—false or broken teeth, blood, vomit, or mucus—that may be blocking the air passage. If this happens, reach into his mouth with your fingers and scoop out the contents fast. If he still doesn't start to breathe, you must start mouth-to-mouth resuscitation immediately.

How do I give mouth-to-mouth resuscitation?

1. Keep the patient's head tilted right back as far as it will go, with the chin jutting up. Place one hand under the neck to lift and support it.
2. Open the patient's mouth.
3. Take a deep breath, and place your mouth tightly over the victim's mouth. Pinch his nostrils firmly shut so that no air can escape. (Or seal his mouth with your hand and put your mouth over his nose.) Blow slowly and deeply. His chest should rise as his lungs fila
4. Take your mouth away and turn your held. to watch the patient's chest fall as the air comes out. By keeping your ear close to his mouth, you may also hear, or feel, the exhaled breath.
5. If the victim doesn't exhale after the first breath, quickly tilt the head further back and try again. Still nothing? Roll the victim on his side and strike him between the shoulder

blades. This may dislodge any obstruction further down in the throat. Wipe his mouth clear and resume mouth-to-mouth breathing.

6. As soon as the casualty has completed an exhaled breath, breathe into his mouth again. Blow again, allow all the air to escape, then begin again. Give the first four breaths as rapidly as possible. After that, continue at a steady, rhythmical rate, in time with the rise and fall of the victim's chest. This will probably mean giving about 10 or 12 breaths per minute. *For babies and small children*, cover both nose and mouth with your mouth, and blow gentle puffs of air—just sufficient to cause the chest to rise. The first 6 to 10 puffs should be given as rapidly as possible. After that, the child will need around 15 to 20 breaths a minute.

7. Continue mouth-to-mouth resuscitation until the casualty is able to breathe freely by himself. His breaths will be weak and shallow at first. Help him along for a while, keeping your breaths in time with his own. When he is breathing strongly and steadily, place him in the coma position (see page 141). Keep checking on his breathing until medical help arrives.

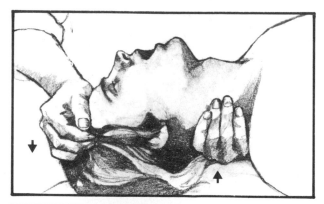

What if he just doesn't start breathing? Is there anything else I can do?

If a person is not breathing, it may be because his heart has stopped. This is particularly likely in cases of severe electric shock. If, in spite of your efforts, the first four breaths produce no result, continue to give mouth-to-mouth resuscitation, but between breaths, check that his heart is beating.

How can I tell if his heart has stopped beating?

Feel for the pulse to the side of, and behind, the Adam's apple. If you can feel no pulse, the heart has stopped. The patient will be blue-gray in color and his pupils will be dilated.

What should I do if the heart has stopped?

Strike the chest smartly over the heart. This may be enough to start the beat. If not, quickly place the heel of one hand on the lower half of the breastbone and cover it with the heel of the other hand. Press down firmly on the lower

Method of giving mouth-to-mouth resuscitation. Top left: bending the patient's head back to clear his air passages. Center left: breathing into the patient's mouth while pinching his nostrils shut to prevent any air escaping. Bottom left: watching the patient's chest fall as the breath is exhaled.

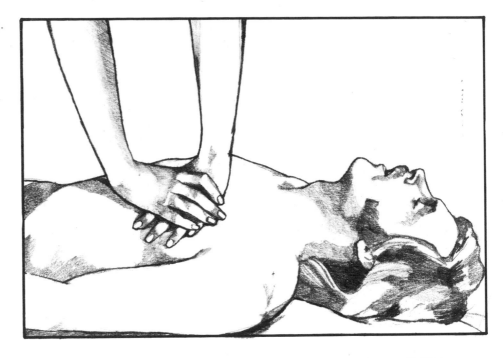

Right: restarting the heart by pressing down on the lower part of the patient's breastbone.

part of the breastbone by rocking forward with your arms straight. Do this about once a second for an adult. *For a child*, use one hand only and press more rapidly—about 80 times a minute. *For a baby*, use finger tips only and press 100 times a minute. Meanwhile, you must continue giving mouth-to-mouth resuscitation. If you are alone, alternate two inflations of the lungs by mouth-to-mouth breathing with 15 heart compressions. Counting aloud will help you. If you have help, one person should do mouth-to-mouth breathing only; the other should do the heart compressions. The two of you should not act simultaneously, but alternate one air inflation with six heart compressions.

How long should I go on giving lung-heart resuscitation?

If the heart has restarted, the patient's color will improve strikingly. His pulse will return and his pupils will become smaller. Continue pressing on the heart until this happens. Carry on giving mouth-to-mouth resuscitation until the casualty is able to breathe of his own accord. It may be necessary to continue lung-heart resuscitation, or mouth-to-mouth breathing alone, for an hour—or even considerably longer. Never give up until you can hand the patient over to a doctor.

What if I am alone in the house? How can I give mouth-to-mouth resuscitation and call help?

A person who is not breathing cannot be left for even a minute without mouth-to-mouth resuscitation. But once a supply of oxygen has been established, it is possible to stop mouth-to-mouth breathing for 15 seconds. So continue mouth-to-mouth breathing for 5 minutes—judge this by counting 60 breaths for an adult, 75 for a child. Meanwhile, think of the quickest way to call help. A neighbor? Passers-by in the street? Or the telephone? Choose the nearest. In between each breath, try to drag the person, bit by bit, to door, window or telephone. Stop mouth-to-mouth breathing for 10 seconds while you open the door. Continue respiration for 20 breaths, then shout for help. Go on shouting between every 20 breaths. If you choose the telephone, get it on the floor and dial between every 20 breaths. Call for an ambulance and continue mouth-to-mouth breathing until it arrives.

Can I practice mouth-to-mouth resuscitation on members of my family?

While it is a good idea to practice techniques such as bending the head right back to unblock breathing, it is not wise to give mouth-to-

135

mouth resuscitation to someone who is breathing normally. Far better for you, and your family, to take a short first aid course, where you can learn how to give mouth-to-mouth resuscitation in less than half-an-hour.

Falls and Fractures

How dangerous is it for a child to fall on his head?

It's very common for babies to fall on their heads—a frightening accident for mothers, although the baby rarely comes to any harm. Similarly, children often bang their heads quite hard without doing any serious damage. But since such injuries can be serious, it is best to know the danger signals, just in case.

How can I tell if the child is seriously hurt? And what should I do if he is?

If a child is knocked right out by a blow on the head (even for a second or two), or if he loses consciousness later, you should call for medical help immediately. Check the child's breathing, clear any obstructions from his mouth, and keep him lying on his side until help arrives. Usually, however, after a blow on the head, the child will start screaming, probably more from fright than pain. Quickly check that there is no food in his mouth that could choke him and then take him in your arms and comfort him. While you hold him, examine his head gently. Any bleeding from the ears or nose could indicate serious injury and needs immediate medical help. If the child has cut his head, stop the bleeding by direct pressure. (Wounds in the scalp, even superficial ones, tend to bleed a lot, but pressure will control the bleeding until the child is better and you can wash the cut or decide whether it needs medical treatment.) If the child stops crying within 15 minutes, keeps a good color, and seems his usual self again, he is almost certainly all right. Possibly he will fall asleep, worn out with crying. If so, it is wise to wake him before you lay him down to make sure he is still normally conscious. If he remains asleep, check once or twice during the next hour or so to see that he is sleeping normally. If anything about his appearance or behavior worries you, call the doctor. Sometimes, after a more severe blow on the head, a child may vomit, remain pale for several hours, lose his appetite and continue to show signs of headache. This may be no cause for alarm, but it is wise to consult your doctor. Symptoms that always call for medical attention are vomiting some time after the accident, continued headache, unusual drowsiness, or blurred vision.

What exactly is concussion, and how can I recognize it?

Concussion is a shaking up and bruising of the brain following a knock-out blow to the head. A victim of concussion will lose consciousness after the blow, but will often recover fairly quickly. However, there is a danger that the blow which knocked him out may also have damaged his brain and this may be serious if not treated. If this happens, the victim of concussion will slowly lose consciousness again—possibly as long as several hours after the accident—and will not recover unless he gets medical help. That is why it is vital for anyone who blacks out, even momentarily, after a head injury, to be examined by a doctor, even if he seems to have recovered. As long as this precaution is taken, concussion rarely causes any lasting damage.

How can I tell if a bone is fractured?

Inability to move the injured part, pain, and swelling or misshapenness may indicate a fracture, or you may be able to see the end of a broken bone poking through the skin. Often, however, there are no symptoms beyond swelling and pain, and a fracture can easily be mistaken for a sprain or even a bad bruise. For this reason, it is safest to treat any injury that causes pain or swelling around a bone as a fracture and keep any pressure off it until you can get medical advice.

How should I treat a fracture?

In any situation where you suspect a fracture, do not move the injured person at all, even to make him more comfortable. If he is bleeding, stem the flow of blood, but do not try to push a protruding bone back into place. Cover any wound, place a coat or blanket over the casualty and summon medical help. On no account, bundle him into the back of a car to get him to hospital. Time won't make the injury worse but moving the patient may. If the person *must* be moved—perhaps because he is threatened by further danger—he should be moved by two people. One should hold the injured limb in exactly the position in which it is, while the other lifts the casualty onto a flat, hard surface that will support the injured part. If—and only if—it is essential to move the patient any distance before he can see a doctor, you must first prevent the injured limb from moving. This is best done by strapping the limb to the patient's body. In the case of a broken arm, strap it gently to the patient's side with scarves, belts or any other available material. (If the arm can be bent without pain, use a sling.) For an injured leg, tie both legs gently together. Always remember to tie above and below the break, not over it. Never, never move a person who appears to have neck, spinal, or skull injuries (beyond getting him out of the path of immediate danger, when he must have something firm beneath his back to keep it straight). Moving him wrongly could cause permanent damage, paralysis, or even death. Keep him still, keep him warm, and keep a watch on his breathing. Do not give a fracture victim anything to eat or drink, as he may need an anesthetic when the bone is set.

Burns and Scalds

What is meant by first-, second-, and third-degree burns?

This is a way of classifying burns according to the depth of damage they cause. In a first degree burn, there is a reddening of the skin caused by the swelling of small blood vessels, but the skin remains unbroken. In a second-degree burn, fluid escapes from the swollen blood vessels into the skin and causes blisters. In a third-degree burn, the skin and some of the tissues beneath it are destroyed. More important than the depth of the burn, however, is its extent. An extensive burn that affects a large area of the body's surface is dangerous, regardless of its depth.

Why is an extensive burn more dangerous than a deep one? Can such a burn be fatal?

The chief danger of a burn lies in the loss of fluid through the damaged skin. This fluid, which is known as *plasma*, comes from the bloodstream and contains a number of important chemicals. Its loss reduces the supply of blood to the brain and may thus cause a form of shock which could be fatal. The fluid lost from a small burn may not be more than a thimbleful and will cause no harm. But in a large burn, several pints of fluid may be lost, and the greater the surface affected, the more fluid will escape. In an extensive burn, therefore, it may be necessary to replace the lost fluid by a transfusion of plasma or plasma substitute. Another possible cause of death from burns is infection. Here again, the larger the surface, the more germs are able to enter the body.

How extensive does a burn have to be before fluid loss becomes dangerous?

Doctors estimate that when more than 15 per cent of the skin area of the body is burned, the fluid loss becomes serious. The skin covering the back or front of the trunk, or a leg, for example, represents about 18 per cent of the body's total skin area. Anyone burned over the chest and abdomen, or the back, or the whole of one limb, should therefore receive urgent hospital treatment.

Is the injury to the body the same in a scald?

Yes. It is the heat that causes the damage, and injury to the skin and body is the same whether caused by dry heat, as in a burn, moist heat, as in a scald, or corrosive chemicals such as sulfuric acid or caustic soda.

What should I do if someone is badly burned or scalded?

In a severe burn, immediately cover the burned area with sterile gauze or clean sheeting, and get to the hospital without delay. If you have no car available, call an ambulance. While waiting for an ambulance, give the injured person frequent, small drinks of cold water with no more than a ¼ teaspoonful of salt and a ¼ teaspoonful of bicarbonate of soda to each glass, to replace body fluids. Flavor the drink with fruit juice if you can—Vitamin C will aid healing. Treat for shock (see page 132). Do not remove any burned clothing which has cooled, as this will already have been rendered sterile, and leave any blisters alone, for while the skin remains intact over the blister, germs cannot get in. Don't apply iodine, ointments, lotions, oils, or any antiseptic to a severe burn. The drugs in these may be absorbed into the body and cause dangerous reactions, or interfere with subsequent medical care.

What if the burn is caused by a chemical?

Immediately rinse the chemical off the person's skin with large amounts of cold water. Put him in the shower if necessary. Cut away any affected clothing, being careful not to burn yourself. Cover the burned area lightly with a sterile dressing or clean, dry cloth, and summon, or get to, medical help. Meanwhile, follow the same treatment as for severe burns.

How should I treat mild burns or scalds?

Immerse the burned area in cold running water to cool it and to relieve pain. Allow the area to dry and cover it loosely with a sterile gauze bandage or a clean cloth. Use specially packaged gauze impregnated with petroleum jelly if you have it. This helps prevent any blisters from breaking and guards against infection. Remember not to tamper with blisters, and don't use any other cream—not even a burn ointment.

Why shouldn't I use a burn ointment?

Leading authorities on the treatment of burns maintain that most proprietary burn ointments appear to be of no greater value in relieving pain than a simple petroleum jelly (which is a basic constituent of many such ointments anyway). It has not been established, they say, whether or not burn ointments prevent infection or promote healing. But, in some cases, the ointments may interfere with healing or set up allergic reactions. Their advice, therefore, is not to use a burn ointment.

What are the dangers of scarring from a burn?

Scarring depends, of course, on the severity of the burn. Most of us have suffered occasional burns from a hot stove and know that these fade away in time. At the other extreme, tissue destroyed by a very severe burn may have to be replaced by skin grafts. However, some doctors have found that Vitamin C is highly successful in relieving pain and healing even severe burns without scarring.

Poisoning

What is a poison?

Any substance which, when taken in sufficient quantity, can kill or damage the body, is considered to be a poison—even everyday foods if eaten to excess. The really dangerous poisons, however, are substances that harm or kill in relatively small quantities.

What are these substances? How much of them would be harmful?

Dangerous poisons may include alcohol or other drugs that can be used safely in moderate doses, or substances that were never meant to be swallowed, such as corrosive chemicals, household cleansers, pesticides, poisonous berries, or bad food. The amount needed to do any harm varies. Ten or 12 aspirins, gulped down in quick succession, could be fatal. So could 9 or 10 large whiskies. Less than a couple of ounces of some chemicals or of poisonous fungi or berries may be highly dangerous. Children, of course, with their smaller capacities, are more at risk than adults from poisoning. Four or 5 adult aspirin tablets (around 16 junior aspirin) might endanger the life of a child. And even a single cigarette eaten by an infant could be dangerous.

What effect do these poisons have on the body? How can I tell if someone has swallowed a poison?

An overdose of drugs or alcohol affects the central nervous system. This may disrupt brain signals to the lungs until the victim stops breathing and his heart ceases to beat. Symptoms of an overdose of aspirin, tranquilizers, barbiturates (sleeping tablets), or heroin may include stomach pain and nausea, extreme sleepiness, unconsciousness, pinpointed pupils, sweating, blue skin, gasping, and either deep, snoring breathing, or very rapid shallow breathing. Too much alcohol causes confusion, uncoordinated movements, enlarged pupils, and unconsciousness, and the victim will, of course, smell of drink. Remember, alcohol and barbiturates taken together are a particularly dangerous combination, each reinforcing the effect of the other. Corrosives, such as bleach, ammonia, disinfectant, and other strong acids or alkalis, burn the mouth, gullet, and stomach. Someone who has swallowed a corrosive is likely to complain of intense pain all the way down to his stomach. His lips and mouth may already be burned yellow, gray, or white, and you may be able to smell the substance on his breath. Some other poisons, such as poisonous plants and berries or bad food, act directly on the food passage, causing vomiting, pain, and often diarrhea. Any of these symptoms should alert you to the possibility of poisoning. Then, of course, there are the obvious clues: an empty or half-empty bottle of tablets or alcohol, a container of household chemicals, or a syringe, for example.

Supposing I find my child playing with an open container of tablets or household chemicals. What should I do?

Quickly remove any tablets that may still be in the child's mouth. If possible, ask him calmly how many tablets he has eaten. Check the container to see what he has swallowed. Then telephone your doctor. If he is not immediately available, call the nearest Poison Control Center (all centers are open 24 hours a day). Remember to take the container with you to the telephone, so that you can read out the contents on the label. If you have a car, drive the child to the nearest hospital, being sure to take the container of tablets or chemicals with you and any vomit for analysis.

Supposing I have to wait for medical help. Is there anything I can do in the meantime? Should I make the child vomit to get rid of the poison, for example?

The treatment for poisoning depends on the kind of poison that has been taken. That is why it is important to get advice from your doctor or Poison Control Center and follow it to the letter. Many of the poisons a child may swallow are not immediately harmful, and since being treated for poisoning can be very frightening, it is best left to a doctor whenever possible. However, if you have been advised to treat the child yourself, or if you have to wait as long as 10 or 15 minutes for an ambulance, you may have to take action on your own. This may mean making the child vomit, or doing all you can to prevent him vomiting, according to the substance he has swallowed.

What are the poisons that should NOT be vomited?

Do not make the child vomit if he has swallowed a corrosive substance or a petroleum product (ammonia, bleach, disinfectant, drain cleaner, lye, oven cleaner, rust remover, any kind of strong acid or alkali, styptic pencil, toilet bowl cleaner, washing soda, or any other cleaning fluid, benzene, kerosene, lighter fluid, gasoline, metal or furniture polish, turpentine, spot remover, typewriter or gun cleaner, or wood preservative. Many pesticides, insecticides, and rat poisons also contain harsh acids or alkalis—check the label). Any of these substances burn the lining of the stomach, and, if vomited, may cause further burning or be inhaled into the lungs with fatal results. The best way to counteract the harmful effect of these poisons is to dilute them by giving drinks of water or milk—aim at 3 or 4 glasses, but only give him as much as he can manage. Do not give any fluids if the child is already unconscious or having convulsions.

Which poisons should be vomited?

If—and only if—you are certain the child has not been poisoned by a corrosive or petroleum product, try to make him vomit. This is especially advisable if he has taken aspirin, sleeping tablets, tranquilizers, or other drugs—*unless he is already half asleep or unconscious*. To induce vomiting, use syrup of ipecac—a package of this, with ready-measured doses, should always be in your medicine chest. Above all, do not give the child salt water to make him vomit. Too much salt can be a poison in its own right. It may seriously upset the salt balance in a child's body, or even react harmfully with the poison he has swallowed. If you have no syrup of ipecac, give the child a drink of carbonated beverage or milk, turn him over on his stomach with his head down, and tickle the back of his throat with your fingers. Have a basin at the ready, as the doctor will need to examine the vomit later. If medical help is still not available, repeat the process a couple more times. When the child has finished vomiting, wrap him up warmly and comfort him—he will be very frightened. If possible, give him a tablespoonful of powdered activated charcoal, or "Universal Antidote," stirred into half a glass of warm water. This will neutralize any poison still remaining in the stomach. Even if the child seems to have vomited all the poison, you must still consult a doctor. Some poisons, such as aspirin, may have a serious delayed effect—possibly several hours later.

Supposing I don't know what poison my child has swallowed. Should I make him vomit or not?

Provided the child is conscious, the best treatment for an unknown poison is the "universal antidote" already mentioned. This is a mixture of two parts powdered activated charcoal, one part tannic acid, and one part magnesium oxide. It can be bought, already made up, from any pharmacy, and should be prominently located in your medicine chest. If no antidote is available, make a solution of one part strong tea, one part milk of magnesia, and two parts crumbled burned toast. Or give water or milk to dilute the poison.

What should I do if I find someone already unconscious, say from an overdose of drugs?

First, check to see if he is breathing. If not, give mouth-to-mouth resuscitation until you can get medical help. If he is unconscious but still breathing, place him in the coma position (below, right), cover him with a blanket and get him to hospital as fast as you can, together with any evidence that might identify the drug taken. Do not give any fluids—these could choke and kill him. Only hospital treatment will save someone who is unconscious as a result of taking an overdose of drugs.

Unconsciousness

What makes a person pass out?

Unconsciousness occurs when the brain is unable to function properly, either because it is not getting enough oxygen or enough blood, or because it is injured by an accident or disease. Unconsciousness may therefore be caused by many different conditions, including blocked breathing, head or other injuries, heavy bleeding and shock, electric shock, lowering of blood sugar levels as in diabetes or insulin shock, heart attack, stroke, epilepsy, convulsions, or poisoning.

How can I revive someone who is unconscious?

The vital first step is to make sure that the casualty can breathe. The greatest danger in unconsciousness (from whatever cause) is the risk of death by choking. Doctors report that more accident victims die from choking while unconscious than from their original injury. An unconscious person is unable to do anything to help himself. His tongue may fall backward and block his throat. False or knocked-out teeth may also block his breathing. Because he cannot cough, spit, or swallow, blood, vomit, or even saliva may choke him. These risks are very much greater if the casualty is lying on his back. So, when you find someone unconscious, quickly check that his mouth is clear of anything that could block the air passages, and bend his head firmly backward as far as it will go. In this position, the tongue cannot block the throat. If the casualty has stopped breathing, immediately start mouth-to-mouth resuscitation. Control any bleeding by direct pressure. Once you are sure he is breathing, place him in the "coma position".

What is the "coma position"?
This is a position that should be used for any patient who is unconscious but breathing—unless serious injury prevents his being moved. Place the patient on his side, with his upper leg and arm bent in front of him so that he cannot roll back. In this position, his head will be inclined downward. The jaw will sag forward so that the tongue cannot fall back into the throat. Any blood, vomit, or fluid will also come forward and run safely out of his mouth. Cover the patient with a blanket or coat, and keep him in this coma position until medical help arrives. If the person cannot be moved because of injury, continue to keep his airway clear by bending his head as far back as it will go, and continue to watch his breathing.

What if the person has merely fainted?
Fainting that follows severe blood loss or serious injury is a sign of shock and should be treated as such (see page 132). If you are in any doubt at all about the reasons for the faint, use the same treatment as for unconsciousness. But if the cause of fainting is obvious—an emotional upset, getting up too soon after an illness, standing for too long in a crowded atmosphere, for example—simply lay the person down with his head turned to one side and his legs raised. Loosen any tight clothing and ensure that he gets plenty of fresh air. As he revives, be calm and reassuring but firm in advising him to rest for a few minutes before getting up again. If he has not fully recovered within five minutes, call the doctor. Laying the patient down is always best, but if this isn't possible, sit him down with his head between his knees until he recovers.

What about giving him a glass of brandy to bring him around?
A person who is unconscious, for whatever reason, should *never* be given anything at all to drink or eat. Remember, he cannot swallow. Any liquid you give him will pass into his lungs and may easily choke him.

Supposing I should find my husband, or child, unconscious following an electric shock. What should I do?
Above all, don't touch him, or you may receive the same shock. Instead, immediately unplug the wire of the appliance involved, or shut off the house current switch. If this is impossible, stand on the nearest dry insulating material you can find (thickly-folded newspaper, wood, or a large book), and drag the person away from the wire with a dry, nonconductive object (a broomstick, chair, shoe, or more books). Don't use an umbrella—it has metal ribs. An electric shock from the current in the average home may be severe enough to paralyze the part of the brain that controls breathing and stop the

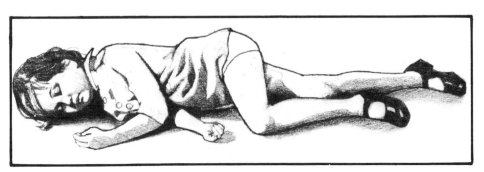

The coma position, used to help an unconscious person to breathe more easily and protect him from the risk of choking.

heart. So, when the person is clear of the wire, you may need to begin mouth-to-mouth resuscitation and heart compression. Keep this up—no matter how long it takes—until he can be got to a hospital. If he is breathing, treat for unconsciousness and shock and call help.

Heart Attack and Stroke

What exactly is a heart attack? How does it happen?

Heart attack is another name for *coronary thrombosis*, or a blockage in the arteries that supply blood to the heart. Although the attack is sudden, the conditions that cause it have been building up for years beforehand. As we grow older, changes occur in the inner lining of the arteries and they tend to thicken. In addition, fatty material from the blood may be laid down inside the arteries, thus narrowing the channel. Parts of this material may flake off, contributing to blockage and roughening the arterial wall. The narrowed channel slows down the flow of blood and where the wall is roughened, a blood clot may form. The clot, called a *thrombus*, cuts off the blood supply to part of the heart, and the heart attack occurs. If the clot blocks a major artery, the attack is likely to be fatal, because without blood the heart will stop beating. If the blockage is less serious, however, blood may find its way around the blocked artery to reach the heart through other blood vessels.

What are the symptoms of a heart attack?

A serious heart attack causes sudden severe and crushing pain in the center of the chest, sometimes radiating down the arms or into the neck and back. The pain may bring on breathlessness, dizziness, and vomiting. The person will be deathly pale, may break out in a cold sweat, and collapse or lose consciousness.

What should I do if someone has a heart attack?

Send for the doctor immediately. If he is not available right away, call an ambulance. Meanwhile, treat the patient for shock (see page 132), but keep him in a sitting position, with his head and shoulders supported by pillows or cushions, so that he can breathe more easily. Try to keep him as calm and quiet as possible, reassuring him that medical help is on its way. Do not give him any medicines or other drink. Watch him carefully and if his breathing stops, immediately start mouth-to-mouth resuscitation and heart compression (see pages 134-5).

What are the chances of recovery from a heart attack?

The majority of heart attacks are not fatal. And if a person recovers from a heart attack, he stands every chance of living a reasonably long and healthy life. One heart attack does not inevitably lead to another. The heart has great powers of recuperation, which can be helped along by modern medical treatment, and it may become as strong as ever after an attack. It is important, however, to deal with the conditions that led to the attack, and anyone who has suffered a heart attack must follow his doctor's advice concerning diet, exercise, and other aspects of his general health.

What happens in a stroke?

A stroke is similar to a heart attack in that it results from the blockage of an artery—in this case to the brain rather than the heart. The commonest type of stroke, called *cerebral thrombosis*, is also due to the formation of a blood clot in an artery (this time in the brain) that has been damaged by deposits of fatty material. Another kind of stroke is caused by the leakage of a weak blood vessel in the brain. The resulting shortage, or blockage, of the blood supply to the brain interferes with the normal functioning of the brain and may affect the control of movement, sensation, speech, or other bodily functions. Like a heart attack, a stroke may be fatal, or a timely warning that serious trouble could occur if certain health measures are not taken. In the majority of strokes, the symptoms disappear after a few weeks. Sometimes, a stroke may leave a permanent handicap, but this can often be overcome with the help of therapy.

How can I tell if someone is having a stroke?

A severe stroke may cause headache, nausea, confusion, slurred speech, and sudden or gradual loss of consciousness. One side of the person's face, or the limbs on one side of his body may become weak or paralysed. In a mild attack, the patient may simply appear to falter and go momentarily blank.

What should I do to help?

Call a doctor or ambulance immediately. Meanwhile, make sure that the person is breathing· If not, give mouth-to-mouth resuscitation. Remove dentures or any other obstruction that may block breathing, and check that the patient has not injured himself in the fall. Leave him where he has fallen but slip a pillow or cushion under his head. If he is unconscious, or loses consciousness later, place him in the coma position (see page 141). Do not give him anything to eat or drink. Loosen any tight clothing, cover him with a coat or blanket, and keep a careful watch on his breathing until medical help arrives.

General

Can you give me a set of simple rules to follow in the case of an automobile accident?

1. Above all, *do not* pull people out of the car, unless it is already on fire. This could further seriously injure or kill them.
2. Send someone to flag down traffic far enough away from the scene of the accident for safety, or do this yourself. The first cars to come along should be sent in opposite directions to telephone for help. The drivers of any other cars can then act as flagmen to block traffic from both directions.

3. Switch off the ignition and lights in the crashed car to prevent fire.
4. If there is more than one victim, see who needs help most urgently. Give attention first to anyone who is not breathing or who is unconscious, and deal with any severe bleeding. Treat everyone involved for shock (even those who protest that they are "perfectly okay").
5. Even if the crash victims do not appear to be seriously hurt, leave them until help arrives. Anyone thrown on the road should be covered with a coat and guarded from the traffic.

My husband and I are going away for the first time without our children. My parents will be looking after them, but I am worried in case there should be an emergency and one of the children needs medical attention. Don't parents have to sign an authorization allowing such treatment? Supposing our child is ill and we can't be reached?

Don't worry. All you need to do is to leave an authorization for medical treatment, already signed, with your parents before you go away. Here is how such an authorization should read:

TO WHOM IT MAY CONCERN:

As a parent, I do herewith authorize the treatment by a qualified and licensed medical doctor of the following minors in the event of a medical emergency which, in the opinion of the attending physician, may endanger his or her life, cause disfigurement, physical impairment, or undue discomfort if delayed. This authority is granted only after a reasonable effort has been made to reach me.

NAME OF MINORS: RELATION: BIRTH DATE:

———————————   —————   —————

This release form is completed and signed of my own free will with the sole purpose of authorizing medical treatment under emergency circumstances in my absence.

Signed ———————————— (Father)

Signed ———————————— (Mother)

Address ————— Phone ————— Office —————

Family Physician ————————— Phone —————

Special Information for treating physician:
(Allergic to Penicillin, Haemophiliac, etc)

———————————————————————

For Your Bookshelf

Child Sense
by William E. Homan, M.D., Basic Books, Inc. (New York: 1969); Thomas Nelson & Sons Ltd. (London: 1970)

Your Child from 1 to 12
with a foreword by Lee Salk, PhD., Signet Books, The New American Library, Inc. (New York: 1970)

Let's Have Healthy Children
by Adelle Davis, Harcourt Brace Jovanovich, Inc. (New York: 1951, 1959, 1972); George Allen & Unwin Ltd. (London: 1972)

Drugs, Parents, and Children
The Three-Way Connection, by Mitchell S. Rosenthal, M.D. and Ira Mothner, Houghton Mifflin Company (Boston: 1972)

How Not to Die Young
by Joan Gomez, M.D., Stein and Day (New York: 1972)

Help Your Husband Stay Alive
by Hannah Lees, Appleton-Century-Crofts, Inc. (New York: 1957)

Freedom from Heart Attacks
by Benjamin F. Miller, M.D. and Lawrence Galton with Daniel Brunner, M.D., Simon and Schuster, Inc. (New York: 1972)

The Old Person in Your Home
by William D. Poe, M.D., Charles Scribner's Sons (New York: 1969)

The Crowning Years
by Siegmund H. May, M.D., J.B. Lippincott Company (Philadelphia and New York: 1968)

Guide to Modern Medical Care
by Solomon D. Klotz, M.D., Charles Scribner's Sons (New York: 1967)

Without Prescription
by Erwin Di Cyan, Ph.D. and Lawrence Hessman, M.D., Simon and Schuster, Inc. (New York: 1972)

The Medicine Show
by the editors of Consumer Reports, Consumers' Union of U.S., Inc. (Mount Vernon, New York: 1971)

The New Concise Family Health and Medical Guide
edited by Richard J. Wagman, M.D., Consulting Editor: N. Henry Moss, M.D., J.G. Ferguson Publishing Company (Chicago: 1971), distributed by Doubleday and Company, Inc.

Picture Credits